New Intensive Japanese

New Intensive Japanese

(REVISED & ENLARGED)

Kenji Ogawa

Associate Professor,
Department of Asian Studies,
University of British Columbia, Canada

Tokyo

THE HOKUSEIDO PRESS

1970

First published 1966

Revised & Enlarged 1970

The Hokuseido Press

12, 3-Chome, Nishikicho, Kanda, Tokyo, Japan

PREFACE

This book, which has evolved from my experience of teaching Japanese to English-speaking students, is intended for both those who desire to learn basic Japanese and those who wish to pursue the study of the language at a more advanced level.

The first part of the book, printed in the conventional Western style, consists of a series of brief lessons, each containing: (A) vocabulary; (B) selected examples; (C) grammatical analysis; (D) conversational expressions. This section is concluded by a chapter on functional Japanese grammar, which supplements the lessons with a summary of other essential points of grammar.

Part Two, printed in the traditional Japanese manner (that is, starting from the back of the book), introduces the student to more advanced aspects of the language through a number of selected passages, each accompanied by a vocabulary and a section on construction patterns.

University of British Columbia,
Canada   Kenji Ogawa

PART ONE

LESSON I

A

kore this	*ja arimasén* is not
hón book	*are* that over there
désu is	*náni* what
sore that	*zasshí* magazine
kamí paper	*tsukue* desk
hái yes	*mo* too; also
isú chair	*iíe* no

B

Kore wa hon desu.
Sore wa kami desu ka?
Hai, sore wa kami desu.
Kore wa isu desu ka?
Iie, kore wa isu ja arimasen.
Are wa isu ja arimasen.
Kore wa nan desu ka?
Sore wa zasshi desu.
Are wa tsukue desu ka, isu desu ka?
Are wa tsukue desu.
Kore mo hon desu.
Sore mo kami desu ka?
Are mo tsukue ja arimasen.

C

1. *Wa* is a postposition indicating that the word or words preceding it is usually in the nominative case.

   Kore wa hon desu.   This is a book.

2. *Ka* placed at the end of a sentence or a phrase denotes interrogation.

   Sore wa nan desu ka?   What is that?

3. *Mo* takes the place of *wa.*

Are mo isu desu.   That over there is also a chair.

4. Japanese nouns have no number and, as a rule, no gender. Singularity or plurality of a noun is determined by the context.

D

Ohayō gozaimasu.	Good morning.
Konnichi wa.	Good afternoon.
Konban wa.	Good evening.
Oyasumi nasai.	Good night.
Sayo nara.	Goodbye.

LESSON II

A

watakushi	I	*Kanadájin*	Canadian
anáta	you	*Nihonjín*	Japanese
-san	Mr.; Miss; Mrs.	*Amerikájin*	American
sō (óo)	so	*gakusei*	student
ano kata	he; she	*senséi*	teacher
		dónata	who

B

Watakushi wa Yamakawa desu.
Anata wa Jōnzu-san desu ka?
Iie, sō ja arimasen.

Ano kata wa Kanadajin desu ka?
Hai, sō desu.
Ikeda-san wa Nihonjin desu ka, Amerikajin desu ka?
Ikeda-san wa Nihonjin desu.

Anata wa gakusei desu.

Jōnzu-san mo gakusei desu ka?
Horando-san wa gakusei desu ka, sensei desu ka?
Horando-san wa gakusei ja arimasen. Sensei desu.
Anata wa donata desu ka?

C

1. When referring to yourself, the suffix *san* should not be used.
2. *Ja arimasen* becomes *de wa arimasen* in less colloquial speech.
3. The word *watakushi* is often contracted to *watashi* and *atashi* (women only) in colloquial speech.
4. *Ano hito* is less polite than *ano kata.*
5. *Dare* is a less polite substitute for *donata.*

D

Ogenki desu ka?	How are you?
Okagesama de genki desu.	Fine, thank you.
Sore wa kekkō desu.	That's fine. Glad to hear that.
Sore wa ikemasen ne.	That's too bad. Sorry to hear that.

LESSON III

A

akái	red	*enpitsu*	pencil
shirói	white	*mijikái*	short
ō(oó)kii	big	*chiisai*	small
hako	box	*kiíroi*	yellow
nagái	long		

B

Kore wa akai hon desu.
Sore wa shiroi kami desu ka?

Are wa ōkii hako ja arimasen.

Kore mo nagai enpitsu desu ka?
Sore mo mijikai enpitsu desu.
Are mo chiisai hako ja arimasen.

Kore wa akai enpitsu desu ka, kiiroi enpitsu desu ka?
Sore wa akai enpitsu desu. Kiiroi enpitsu ja arimasen.

C

1. There are two kinds of adjectives in Japanese; namely, true adjectives and quasi-adjectives. The true adjectives end in *ai, ii, ui,* or *oi.* The quasi-adjectives are to be dealt with later.

D

Arigatō gozaimasu.   Thank you.
Dō itashimashite.   Not at all.
Ja mata.   See you later.

LESSON IV

A

samúi cold
sámuku arimasén is not cold
atsúi hot
kono this (before a noun)
aói blue
sono that (before a noun)
ano that over there (before a noun)

kaban suitcase
kurói black
takái expensive
yasúi cheap
hankachi hand-kerchief

B

Honoruru wa samui desu ka?
Iie, samuku arimasen. Atsui desu.
Arasuka wa atsui desu ka?

Iie, atsuku arimasen.

Kono hon wa akai desu ka?
Iie, akaku arimasen. Aoi desu.
Sono hako wa ōkii desu ka?
Iie, ōkiku arimasen. Chiisai desu.
Ano kaban wa kuroi desu ka, shiroi desu ka?
Kuroi desu.
Sono ōkii hon wa takai desu ka, yasui desu ka?
Takai desu.
Kono hankachi wa shiroi desu ka?
Kono enpitsu wa nagaku arimasen ka?
Hai, nagaku arimasen.

C

1. The negative form of true adjectives is obtained by changing *i* into *ku* followed by *arimasen*. Sometimes *wa* is used before *arimasen*, adding emphasis to the negation.

    Tōkyō wa atsuku arimasen.   Tokyo is not hot.

2. In colloquial speech *n* is often inserted as a sort of sentence softner between true adjectives or verbs and *desu*.

    Kono hako wa ōkii n desu.   This box is large.

3. The usages of *Hai* and *Iie* in answering a negative question will strike you as strange. If the speaker agrees with the questioner, he says *Hai* regardless of whether there is a negative word in his answer or not. If he does not agree with the questioner, he uses *Iie.*

4. It is an established practice among the Japanese people to omit the subject in everyday speech, provided there is no danger of being misunderstood.

5. Japanese adjectives have no gender or number.

D

Sō desu ka?	Is that so?
Dōzo.	Please.
Ii desu ka?	Is it good?
Dame desu.	That's no good.

LESSON V

A

watakushi no	my	*dónna*	what kind
kutsú	shoe	*iró*	color
anáta no	your	*mannénhitsu*	fountain-pen
uwagi	coat	*bōshi*	cap; hat
zubón	trousers		

B

Watakushi no kutsu wa kuroi desu.
Anata no uwagi wa aoi desu ka?
Iie, aoku arimasen.
Jōnzu-san no zubon wa donna iro desu ka?
Jōnzu-san no zubon wa kuroi desu.

Ano kata no mannenhitsu wa akaku arimasen ka?
Hai, akaku arimasen. Kuroi desu.
Ano kata no bōshi wa donna iro desu ka?

Anata no kutsu wa kuroi desu ne.
Watakushi no kutsu mo kuroi desu.
Ano kata no kutsu mo shiroku arimasen.

C

1. The postposition *no* denotes possession and corresponds to 'of' in English.

2. *Nē* which is equivalent to 'isn't it?', 'is it?' in English is used in inviting the listener to agree with the speaker. *Ne* is used in place of *nē* for making sure that the listener follows the speaker right.

D

Atsui desu ne.	Hot, isn't it?
Samui desu ne.	Cold, isn't it?
Atatakai desu ne.	Warm, isn't it?

LESSON VI

A

anáta no	yours	*dónata no*	whose
watakushi no	mine	*tokei*	watch; clock
jibiki	dictionary		

B

Kore wa anata no desu ka?
Hai, watakushi no desu.
Sono hon wa watakushi no desu ka?
Iie, anata no ja arimasen.
Kono jibiki wa donata no desu ka?
Ishiyama-san no desu.
Ano tokei wa kono kata no desu ka?
Iie, kono kata no ja arimasen. Ano kata no desu.

D

Chotto matte kudasai.	Wait a minute, please.
Moshimoshi.	Say. Hello. Excuse me.
Mizu o kudasai.	Give me a glass of water, please.

LESSON VII

A

to   and   séito   pupil

B

enpitsu to kami
sensei to seito

ōkii tsukue to chiisai isu
Kanadajin to Amerikajin to Nihonjin

Kono enpitsu to kami wa donata no desu ka?
Watakushi no desu.
Sensei to seito wa Kanadajin desu ka?
Iie, sensei wa Nihonjin de, seito wa Kanadajin desu.
Kore wa watakushi no hon de, sore wa anata no hon desu.

C

1. *To* is a connective used in combining two or more nouns. Each noun is followed by this *to* except the last.

2. *De* is a connective employed in combining two or more sentences. This *de* replaces the copula *desu* except the last.

D

Mō kekkō desu.   I've had enough, thank you.
Sumimasen.   I'm sorry.
Jōzu desu ne.   You are good at it, aren't you?
Heta desu.   I'm poor at it.

LESSON VIII

A

daigaku university; college	*no náka ni* in the inside of; in
dóko where	*no ué ni* on top of
ni in; at	*no shitá ni* under
arimásu exist; is	*gakkō* school
koko here	*no sóba ni* by the side of
arimasén do not exist; is not	*chikái* near
soko there	*no máe ni* in front of; before
uchi house; home	*kokuban* blackboard
asuko (*asoko*) over there	*no ushiro ni* behind
pokétto pocket	

B

Buritisshu Koronbia Daigaku wa doko ni arimasu ka?
Bankūbā ni arimasu.
Keiō Daigaku wa Bankūbā ni arimasen.

Anata no enpitsu wa koko ni arimasu ka?
Iie, koko ni arimasen.
Watakushi no jibiki wa soko ni arimasu ka?
Iie, arimasen.
Ikeda-san no uchi wa asuko ni arimasu ka?

Watakushi no hankachi wa poketto no naka ni arimasu.
Akai hon wa doko ni arimasu ka?
Tsukue no ue ni arimasu.
Howaito-san no kaban wa isu no ue ni arimasu ka?
Iie, isu no shita ni arimasu.
Anata no uchi wa gakkō no soba ni arimasu ka?
Hai, sō desu. Chikai desu.
Ano kata no zasshi wa tsukue no ue ni arimasu ka, shita ni
    arimasu ka?
Tsukue no ue ni arimasu.

Tsukue wa doko ni arimasu ka?

Tsukue wa anata no mae ni arimasu.
Kokuban wa watakushi no mae ni arimasu ka?
Iie, anata no ushiro ni arimasu.

C

1. The postposition *ni* denotes a place of existence.

2. The verb *arimasu* expresses the existence of inanimate objects.

D

Hontō ni? Really?   *Shirimasen.* I don't know.
Gomen nasai. Pardon me.   *Sore kara.* Then. After that.

LESSON IX

A

shinbun newspaper   *hitótsu* one
nannimo nothing (follow-   *futatsu* two
   ed by negative)   *mittsú* three
heyá room   *yottsú* four
mádo window   *itsútsu* five
íkutsu how many   *depāto* department store
dóa door

B

Tsukue no ue ni shinbun ga arimasu.
Kaban no naka ni nani ga arimasu ka?
Hon to kami to enpitsu ga arimasu.
Isu no shita ni anata no zasshi ga arimasu ka?
Iie, arimasen.
Kono hako no naka ni nani ga arimasu ka?
Nannimo arimasen.

Kono heya ni mado ga ikutsu arimasu ka?

Yottsu arimasu.
Doa mo yottsu arimasu ka?
Iie, doa wa yottsu arimasen.   Futatsu arimasu.
Bankūbā ni depāto ga ikutsu arimasu ka?
Bankūbā ni depāto ga mittsu arimasu.

C

1. *Ga* is a postposition which indicates that the word or words preceding it is in the nominative case. The difference between *wa* and *ga* is a constant puzzle to students. The fundamental difference between the two particles is that *ga* emphasizes the subject of a sentence, whereas *wa* emphasizes the predicate.

This *is a book.*   *Kore* wa *hon desu.*

This is the book (for which   *Kore* ga *hon desu.*
you are looking, or to which
you referred).

2. Ordinarily numerals are placed after nouns. No particles are used after numerals.

Tsukue ga mittsu arimasu.   There are three desks.

3. The word *nani* when placed before a word which begins with *t, d,* or *n* becomes *nan.*

D

Shitte imasu ka?   Do you know?
Kamaimasen.   Never mind.
Wakarimasu ka?   Do you understand?
Wakarimasen.   I don't understand.

LESSON X

A

kabin vase	*shízuka-na* quiet
kírei-na beautiful	*muttsú* six
haná flower	*nanátsu* seven
anatagata you (plural)	*yattsú* eight
takusán many; a lot	*kokónotsu* nine
yakamashíi noisy	*tō (óo)* ten

B

Kabin no naka ni kirei-na hana ga arimasu.
Kono hana wa kirei desu nē.
Akai hana wa ikutsu arimasu ka?
Muttsu arimasu.
Shiroi hana mo muttsu arimasu ka?
Iie, muttsu arimasen. Yattsu arimasu.

Watakushi wa Nihonjin desu ga, anatagata wa Kanadajin desu.
Tsukue wa hitotsu arimasu ga, isu wa takusan arimasu.
Tōkyọ wa yakamashii desu ga, Bankūbā wa shizuka desu.
Nyūyōku wa shizuka ja arimasen ga, Washinton wa shizuka desu.

C

1. Quasi-adjectives are obtained by adding *na* to abstract nouns. When used predicatively, this *na* must be dropped.

2. *Ga* means 'but', when used in connecting two or more clauses. Sometimes it means 'and'. The context determines whether it means 'but' or 'and'.

D

Oboete imasu ka?	Do you remember?
Oboete imasen.	I don't remember.
Wasuremashita.	I've forgotten it.

LESSON XI

A

ohashi chopsticks	*mimí* ear
de by; with	*kikimásu* hear
tabemásu eat	*kuchí* mouth
osáji spoon	*te* hand
kōhī coffee; *kōcha* tea	*hana* nose
nomimásu drink	*nióí* scent; odor
nomimasén do not drink	*kagimásu* smell (**v.**)
tegami letter	*iroiro no* various
kakimásu write	*monó* things
Eigo English	*mochimásu* hold
hanashimásu speak	*ashí* leg; foot
Furansugo French	*arukimásu* walk
watakushítachi we	*kéredomo* but
me eye	*Supeinjin* Spanish
shimásu do	*Aruzenchínjin* Argentine
mimásu see	*Supeingo* Spanish language

B

Nihonjin wa ohashi de tabemasu.
Kanadajin wa nan de tabemasu ka?
Anata wa osaji de kōhī ya kōcha o nomimasu ka?
Iie, osaji de kōhī ya kōcha o nomimasen.
Enpitsu de tegami o kakimasu ka?
Iie, enpitsu de kakimasen. Pen de kakimasu.

Anata wa Eigo o hanashimasu ka?
Hai, hanashimasu.
Furansugo mo hanashimasu ka?
Hai, Furansugo mo hanashimasu.

Watakushitachi wa me de nani o shimasu ka?
Me de mimasu.
Mimi de nani o shimasu ka?
Mimi de kikimasu.

Kuchi de nani o shimasu ka?
Kuchi de hanashimasu.
Hana de nani o shimasu ka?
Hana de nioi o kagimasu.
Te de nani o shimasu ka?
Iroiro no mono o mochimasu.
Ashi de arukimasu ne.

Kanadajin ya Amerikajin wa Eigo o hanashimasu keredomo,
Supeinjin ya Aruzenchinjin wa Supeingo o hanashimasu.

C

1. *De* is a postposition denoting means or instrument.

2. *Ya* used after each noun except the last in combining two or more nouns differs from *to* in that the list is not given as a complete one.

3. The word or words preceding *o* is in the objective case.

4. *Mo* takes the place of *o* in colloquial Japanese.

5. The present tense in polite or non-plain speech is indicated by *masu*.

6. There are regular and irregular verbs in Japanese. The regular verbs consist of strong verbs and weak verbs. The irregular verbs are limited in number—only three in all.

    The strong verbs (Group I) end in *ku, gu, bu, mu, nu, u, ru, su,* and *tsu.*
    The weak verbs (Group II) end in either *eru* or *iru.*
    There are some strong verbs (Group I) which end in either *eru* or *iru.*

7. Japanese verbs have no person or number.

D

Ojama shimashita.   Sorry to have disturbed you.

	Sorry to have taken too much of your time.
Shikata ga arimasen.	It can't be helped.
Ikura desu ka?	How much is it?
Kore o itadakimasu.	I'll take this.

LESSON XII

A

naraimásu	study; learn	*tokidoki*	sometimes
oshiemásu	teach	*yóku*	well
tomodachi	friend	*sukóshi*	a little

B

Anatagata wa kono gakkō de nani o naraimasu ka?
Watakushitachi wa kono gakkō de Nihongo o naraimasu
Anata wa kono heya de tabemasu ka?
Iie, kono heya de tabemasen.

Horando-san wa anatagata ni Nihongo o oshiemasu ka?
Horando-san wa watakushitachi ni Nihongo o oshiemasen.
Anata wa tomodachi ni tegami o kakimasu ka?
Hai, tokidoki kakimasu.

Anata wa Furansugo ga wakarimasu ka?
Ano kata wa Nihongo ga yoku wakarimasu.
Anatagata wa Nihongo ga sukoshi wakarimasu.

C

1. *De* denotes a place of action. Caution must be used not to confuse it with *ni* which denotes a place of existence.

Shokudō de tabemasu.	We eat in the dining-room.
Shokudō ni arimasu.	It is in the dining-room.

2. The indirect object is indicated by the use of *ni* meaning 'to' in English.

Tomodachi ni tegami o   Do you write letters to
  kakimasu ka?   your friends?

3. An indirect object is ordinarily placed before a direct object.

4. Adverbs are placed before adjectives and verbs.

Sukoshi tabemasu ka?   Do you eat a little?

5. The verb *wakarimasu* demands *ga* or *wa* instead of *o*.

D

Minasan okawari arimasen   How are your folks?
  ka?
Gokurōsama deshita.   Thank you for the trouble.
Otōsan wa ikaga desu ka?   How is your sick father?

LESSON XIII

A

shimáshita did   *ikimasén deshita* did not go
namae name   *íma* now
kakimáshita wrote   *akemáshita* opened
kinō yesterday   *shimemáshita* closed
ikimáshita went

B

Watakushi wa nani o shimashita ka?
Anata wa anata no namae o kakimashita.
Nan de kakimashita ka?
Enpitsu de kakimashita.

Anata wa kinō Bikutoria e ikimashita ka?
Iie, ikimasen deshita.
Watakushi wa ima doa o akemashita ka?
Iie, akemasen deshita. Doa o shimemashita.

C

1. The past tense in polite speech is expressed by *mashita*.

   Tōkyō e ikimashita.　　He went to Tokyo.

2. The negative past of a verb in polite speech is expressed by *masen deshita.*

3. There is no specific form to express the perfect tense.

   Samuku narimashita.　　It has become cold.
   　　　　　　　　　　　　　It became cold.

4. The postposition *e* denotes direction.

   Koko e kite kudasai.　　Come here, please.

D

Doko desu ka?	Where is it?
Dochira e?	Which way are you going?
	Where are you going?
Massugu.	Straight.
Hidari ni magatte kudasai.	Turn to the left, please.
Migi ni arimasu.	It is on your right.

LESSON XIV

A

yóri than	*hō (óo)* side; direction
jidō (óo) sha automobile	*ringo* apple
jiténsha bicycle	*bánana* banana
dótchi which (of the two)	*sukí desu* like

B

Kanada wa Nihon yori ōkii desu.

Bankūbā wa Honoruru yori samui desu ka?

Hai, Bankūbā wa Honoruru yori samui desu.
Jidōsha wa jitensha yori takai desu ka?

Tōkyō to Yokohama to, dotchi ga ōkii desu ka?
Tōkyō wa Yokohama yori ōkii desu.
Tōkyō no hō ga ōkii desu.
Ringo to banana to, dotchi ga yasui desu ka?
Ringo wa banana yori yasui desu.
Ringo no hō ga yasui desu.
Sukiyaki to tenpura to, dotchi ga suki desu ka?
Tenpura no hō ga suki desu.

C

1. Comparison is expressed in the following way:

    (a)   A *to* B *to, dotchi ga* .... *desu ka?*
          A *to* B *ja, dotchi ga* .... *desu ka?*
          Which is ...er, A or B?

    (b)   A *wa* B *yori* .... *desu.*
          A *no hō ga* .... *desu.*
          A *no hō ga* B *yori* .... *desu.*
          A is ...er than B.

2. *Dotchi* (or *dochira*) is used when referring to two things only.

3. *Hō* literally means 'a side' or 'an alternative'.

    Tōkyō no hō ga ōkii desu.   Tokyo is bigger. (Lit. The Tokyo side or alternative is big.)

4. Interrogative pronouns such as *dotchi, dore* (which...?), *donata* (who...?) are followed by *ga,* when used as the subject.

    Dotchi ga ii desu ka?   Which is better?
    Donata ga ikimasu ka?   Who is going?

D

Ohairi kudasai.	Come in, please.
Dōzo kochira e.	This way, please.
Okake kudasai.	Be seated, please.
Ima iki nasai.	Go now.

LESSON XV

A

dóre	which (of more than two)	*hayái*	fast
ichiban	the most	*gyūniku*	beef
atsui	thick	*butaniku*	pork
muzukashii	difficult	*toriniku*	chicken
hikō (óo) ki	airplane	*oishii*	delicious
kishá	train		

B

Jibiki to zasshi to shinbun to, dore ga ichiban atsui desu ka?
Jibiki ga ichiban atsui desu.
Nihongo to Supeingo to Furansugo to, dore ga ichiban muzu-
kashii desu ka?
Nihongo ga ichiban muzukashii desu.
Hikōki to jidōsha to kisha to, dore ga ichiban hayai desu ka?
Hikōki ga ichiban hayai desu.

Gyūniku to butaniku to toriniku to, dore ga ichiban oishii
desu ka?
Gyūniku ga ichiban oishii desu.

C

1. The superlative degree is expressed in the following way:

  (a)   A *to* B *to* C *to, dore ga ichiban ... desu ka?*
        A *to* B *to* C *ja, dore ga ichiban ... desu ka?*

Which is the ...est, A, B or C?

(b) A *ga ichiban* .... *desu.*
    A is the ...est.

2. *Dore* is used when referring to more than two things.

D

Yoku irasshaimashita.	Glad you came.
K-san ni yoroshiku.	Give my regards to Mr. K.
Shitsurei shimashita.	I beg your pardon. Excuse my having been rude.

LESSON XVI

A

sánmai three sheets
minná de in all
nánmai how many sheets
rokúmai six sheets
tabako tobacco; cigarette
nánbon h o w m a n y (cigarettes)
kyō (*óo*) today

nomimásu smoke
gohon five (cigarettes)
nánsatsu how many volumes
nísatsu two volumes
chairo brown color
issoku one pair
máiasa every morning
nánbai how many cups

B

Tsukue no ue ni akai kami ga sanmai arimasu.
Kiiroi kami mo sanmai arimasu.
Minna de nanmai arimasu ka?
Rokumai arimasu.
Hako no naka ni tabako ga nanbon arimasu ka?
Jūnihon arimasu.

Anata wa kyō tabako o nanbon nomimashita ka?

Gohon nomimashita.
Kaban no naka ni hon ga nansatsu arimasu ka?
Nisatsu arimasu.
Isu no shita ni chairo no kutsu ga issoku arimasu.
Maiasa kōhī o nanbai nomimasu ka?

C

1. There are two sets of numerals in Japanese.

1st set		2nd set
hitotsu	one	ichi
futatsu	two	ni
mittsu	three	san
yottsu	four	yon (shi)
itsutsu	five	go
muttsu	six	roku
nanatsu	seven	nana (shichi)
yattsu	eight	hachi
kokonotsu	nine	ku (kyū)
tō	ten	jū

Over ten, the second set of numerals is used.

2. When counting various objects, numeral classifiers should be used with the second set of numerals. When it is difficult to determine the correct counter, the first set of numerals may be used. It may not be correct Japanese, but it is at least intelligible.

3. Counters in common use are:

(a) *Mai* used for thin and flat objects such as sheets of paper, plates, carpets, etc.

(b) *Hon* used for long and thin objects such as pencils, poles, nails, etc.
    ippon, sanbon, roppon, happon, jippon

(c) *Satsu* used for volumes of books, magazines, etc.

issatsu, hassatsu, jissatsu

(d) Soku used for footgear.
     issoku, sanzoku, hassoku, jissoku

(e) Ken used for houses, shops, etc.
     ikken, sangen, rokken, hakken, jikken

(f) Hai used for cupfuls.
     ippai, sanbai, roppai, happai, jippai

(g) Ko used for apples, eggs, boxes, bundles, etc.
     ikko, rokko, hakko, jikko

(h) Tsū used for letters (written messages).
     ittsū, hattsū, jittsū

(i) Hiki used for beasts, insects, fish, etc.
     ippiki, sanbiki, roppiki, happiki, jippiki

(j) Dai used for motorcars, bicycles, machines, etc.

(k) Wa used for birds.
     sanba, jippa

(l) Chaku used for suits, dresses, etc.
     itchaku, hatchaku, jitchaku

(m) Nin used for human beings only (To be treated later).

     Note those euphonic changes which are listed above.

4. As was mentioned previously, numerals are placed after nouns.

     Kami ga nimai arimasu. There are two sheets of paper.
     Mizu o ippai kudasai.   Give me a glass of water, please.

The following will be worth noting:

(a) Gonin no kodomo ga kimashita.
(b) Kodomo ga gonin kimashita.
        (Five children came.)

(a) is more specific about the number referring to the particular children, while (b) is not, the number being only incidental.

D

Mata oide kudasai.   Come again, please.
Sorosoro shitsurei shimashō.   I must be going now.
Dōzo goyukkuri.   Don't hurry away.

LESSON XVII

A

gúrai about; as much as   *hashirimásu* run
hodo about; extent   *suzushíi* cool
néko cat   *sukī* skiing
inú dog   *sukēto* skating
háyaku speedily; fast   *yasashíi* easy

B

Kyōto wa Tōkyō gurai ōkii desu ka?
Iie, Kyōto wa Tōkyō hodo ōkiku arimasen.
Neko wa inu gurai hayaku hashirimasu ka?
Iie, neko wa inu hodo hayaku hashirimasen.

Kyō wa kinō gurai suzushii desu ka?
Hai, kyō wa kinō gurai suzushii desu.
Sukī wa sukēto gurai yasashii desu ka?
Iie, sukī wa sukēto hodo yasashiku arimasen.

C

1. Generally speaking, *gurai* meaning 'as much as' or 'about' is used in an affirmative sentence, whereas *hodo* meaning 'to the extent of' in a negative sentence.

2. Adverbs are formed by changing the final *i* of true adjective into *ku*:

hayai (fast; quick)—*hayaku* (speedily; quickly)
tōi (far)—*tōku* (in the distance)
yoi (good)—*yoku* (well)

3. Quasi-adjectives can be converted into adverbs by replacing *na* or *no* by *ni*:

kirei-na (beautiful)—*kirei-ni* (beatifully)
shizuka-na (quiet)—*shizuka-ni* (quietly)
hontō-no (true)—*hontō-ni* (truly)
tokubetsu-no (special)—*tokubetsu-ni* (specially)

No-ending quasi-adjectives are dealt with later.

4. There are a large number of adverbs which do not end in *ku* or *ni*.

5. Adverbs modify verbs, adjectives and other adverbs.

Totemo oishii n desu.   It is very delicious.
Kanari yoku hanashimasu.   He speaks it fairly well.

D

Mō sukoshi kudasai.   Give me a little more, please.
Tabun.   Maybe.
Daijōbu desu ka?   Is that all right? Are you sure?

LESSON XVIII

A

hito person
nánnin how many people
imásu exist; is

hachínin eight persons
otona grown-ups
kodomo child

minna all	*futari* two persons
otoko no hito man	*otokó no ko* boy
onna no hito woman	*ákachan* baby
hitóri one person	*íkutsu* how many; how old
onná no ko girl	*sō(óo) desu nē* let me see

B

Kono heya ni hito ga nannin imasu ka?
Hachinin imasu.
Otona ga gonin, kodomo ga sannin imasu.
Otona wa minna otoko no hito desu ka?
Iie, futari wa otoko no hito de, sannin wa onna no hito desu.

Kodomo wa minna onna no ko desu ka?
Iie, hitori wa otoko no ko de, futari wa onna no ko desu.
Akachan wa imasen ka?
Hai, imasen.

Ichiban chiisai otoko no ko wa ikutsu gurai desu ka?
Sō desu nē, mittsu gurai desu.

Koko ni Nihonjin ga imasu ka?
Hai, hitori imasu.
Kanadajin wa nannin imasu ka?

C

1. The verb *imasu* expresses the existence of animate objects.

2. *Nin* is a counter used for human beings only.

Note the following irregularity:

hitori	one person	*nananin*	seven persons
futari	two persons	*(shichinin)*	
sannin	three persons	*hachinin*	eight persons
yonin	four persons	*kunin*	nine persons
gonin	five persons	*(kyūnin)*	
rokunin	six persons	*jūnin*	ten persons

D

Sō da to ii desu ne.	I hope so.
Sō ja nai to ii desu ne.	I hope not.
Sō da to omoimasu.	I think so.

LESSON XIX

A

shite (suru) doing
hataraite (hataraku) working
yasúnde (yasumu) resting
kite (kiru) wearing
yōfuku western suit
yónde (yomu) reading
tátte (tatsu) standing
déwa then; if so
migi right
náze why
kara because
haite (haku) wearing
ókusan his or your wife

kákete (kakeru) seated
narátte (narau) learning
hanáshite (hanasu) speaking
kiíte (kiku) hearing
hidari left
te hand
mótte (motsu) holding
hirói wide
michi road
arúite (aruku) walking
nezumiiro no grey
momoiro no pink
zōri sandals

B

Otoko no hito wa nani o shite imasu ka?
Hataraite imasu.
Onna no hito mo hataraite imasu ka?
Iie, hataraite imasen. Yasunde imasu.

Onna no hito wa nani o kite imasu ka?
'Kimono' o kite imasu.
Kodomo wa nani o kite imasu ka?
Yōfuku o kite imasu.

Jōnzu-san wa nani o yonde imasu ka?

Nihon no shinbun o yonde imasu.
Anata wa tatte imasu ka, kakete imasu ka?
Anatagata wa ima nani o shite imasu ka?
Nihongo o naratte imasu.

Watakushi wa hanashite imasu ga, anatagata wa kiite imasu.
Anata wa hidari no te ni nani o motte imasu ka?
Hon o motte imasu.
Dewa, migi no te ni nani o motte imasu ka?
Nanni mo motte imasen.

Anata wa uwagi o kite imasu ka?
Iie, kite imasen.
Naze desu ka?
Atsui kara desu.
Howaito-san wa donna iro no kutsu o haite imasu ka?
Shiroi kutsu o haite imasu.

Ikeda-san to okusan wa hiroi michi o aruite imasu.
Ikeda-san wa nezumiiro no uwagi o kite, chairo no zubon o
    haite, kuroi kutsu o haite imasu.
Ikeda-san no okusan wa momoiro no 'kimono' o kite, shiroi
    zōri o haite imasu.

Watakushi wa nani o shite imashita ka?
Zasshi o yonde imashita.
Anata wa hanashite imashita ka?
Iie, hanashite imasen deshita. Kiite imashita.

C

1.   The *te*-form followed by *imasu* is equivalent to 'to be -ing'
form in English.   It denotes either an action in progress or
a state.   In the case of intransitive verbs, context decides
whether an action in progress or a state is meant.

> *Aruite imasu.*   He is walking. (action)
> *Doa wa aite imasu.*   The door is open. (state)

In the case of transitive verbs, it denotes an action in progress.

Tegami o kaite imasu.	I am writing a letter.
Hon o yonde imashita ka?	Were you reading a book?

2. The formation of this *te*-form is shown below:

   (a)   Group I (Strong Verbs)

2nd base	Dictionary form	*Te*-form
kiki-masu (hear)	*kiku*	*kiite*
yasumi-masu (rest)	*yasumu*	*yasunde*
narai-masu (learn)	*narau*	*naratte*
hanashi-masu (speak)	*hanasu*	*hanashite*
mochi-masu (hold)	*motsu*	*motte*
nugi-masu (undress)	*nugu*	*nuide*
yobi-masu (call)	*yobu*	*yonde*
shini-masu (die)	*shinu*	*shinde*
tori-masu (take)	*toru*	*totte*

The only exception to the above is: *iki-masu* (2nd base), *iku* (Dictionary form), *itte* (*Te*-form).

   (b)   Group II (Weak Verbs)

tabe-masu (eat)	*taberu*	*tabete*
mi-masu (look)	*miru*	*mite*

   (c)   Irregular Verbs

kimasu (come)	*kuru*	*kite*
shimasu (do)	*suru*	*shite*

3. Next to Group I verbs, Group II "eru"-ending verbs make up the largest number of Japanese verbs. Group II "iru"-ending verbs are limited in number. Those "iru"-ending verbs which are in common use are: *miru* (see), *iru* (exist), *kiru* (wear), *okiru* (get up), *dekiru* (be possible), *oriru* (get off), *ochiru* (fall, drop), *shinjiru* (believe), *niru* (cook), *niru* (resemble), *sugiru* (pass), *ikiru* (live), *akiru* (get tired of something).

4.   As was mentioned before, there are some Group I verbs
which end in either *iru* or *eru*.   Those *iru-* or *eru*-ending
verbs which are in common use are as follows:

2nd base	Dictionary form	Te-form
heri-masu (decrease)	*heru*	*hette*
suberi-masu (slip)	*suberu*	*subette*
keri-masu (kick)	*keru*	*kette*
shaberi-masu (chatter)	*shaberu*	*shabette*
teri-masu (shine)	*teru*	*tette*
kaeri-masu (go back)	*kaeru*	*kaette*
hairi-masu (enter)	*hairu*	*haitte*
kiri-masu (cut)	*kiru*	*kitte*
shiri-masu (know)	*shiru*	*shitte*
mairi-masu (go or come)	*mairu*	*maitte*
chiri-masu (scatter)	*chiru*	*chitte*
iri-masu (need)	*iru*	*itte*

5.   The postposition *o* denotes a place of motion.   A place in
which or through which such a motion as walking, running,
passing, flying, etc. occurs is denoted by a noun with the
postposition *o*.

Warui michi o arukimashita.   We walked along the bad road.
Hikōki ga sora o tonde imasu.   An airplane is flying in the air.

6.   Two or more clauses can be combined into a single sentence
by the use of the *te*-form at the end of non-final clause or
clauses.   The verb of the final clause determines the tense.
The verb or adjective at the end of each clause except the
last is put into the *te-form*.

Kaite ikimasu.   I will write it and go.
Sukoshi yasunde kaerimashita.
                He rested a little and went home.
Takakute warui n desu.   It is expensive and of poor quality.
Chiisakute akai deshita ka?   Was it small and red?

7.   *Kara* expressing the reason is placed at the end of a sentence.

D

Nani mo gozaimasen ga.	We don't have much on the table.
Goenryo naku.	Don't stand on ceremony.
Oraku ni.	Make yourself at home, please.
Dōzo meshiagatte kudasai.	Please help yourself.

LESSON XX

A

nánji what time
rokuji-hán 6:30
okimásu (okiru) get up
taitei generally
góro about
ni at
asagóhan breakfast
ohirugóhan lunch
ka or
bangóhan supper
osoku late
ban night; evening
yasumimásu (yasumu) go to bed

kúrasu class
hajimarimásu (hajimaru) begin
owarimásu (owaru) end
átte imásu (au) be correct
susunde imásu (susumu) be fast
okurete imásu (okureru) be slow
nanjíkan how many hours
nemásu (neru) sleep

B

Ima nanji desu ka?
Rokuji-han desu.
Anata wa maiasa nanji ni okimasu ka?
Taitei shichiji goro okimasu.
Nanji ni asagohan o tabemasu ka?
Ohirugohan wa nanji desu ka?
Jūniji ka jūniji-han goro desu.
Kanadajin wa bangohan o osoku tabemasu ka?
Hai, Kanadajin wa Amerikajin yori osoku tabemasu.
Anata wa kinō no ban nanji ni yasumimashita ka?
Jūji jūgofun mae goro yasumimashita.

Asa rokuji ni okite, ban jūji ni yasumimasu.
Kono kurasu wa nanji ni hajimarimasu ka?
Hachiji gofun ni hajimarimasu.
Nanji ni owarimasu ka?
Kuji gofun ni owarimasu.

Anata no tokei wa atte imasu ka?
Sanpun gurai susunde imasu.
Watakushi no tokei wa gofun okurete imasu.
Anata wa nanjikan nemasu ka?
Rokujikan gurai desu.

C

1. Note the following euphonic changes:

ippun	one minute	*roppun*	six minutes
nifun	two minutes	*nanafun*	seven minutes
sanpun	three minutes	*happun*	eight minutes
yonpun	four minutes	*kyūfun*	nine minutes
gofun	five minutes	*jippun*	ten minutes

2. *Goro* meaning 'approximate point in time' is used only in reference to time, whereas *gurai* meaning 'approximate quantity' is used with any word. These words are tacked on to the end of a number (after the counter).

Hachiji gofun-sugi goro kite kudasai. Please come about 8:05.
Gofun gurai matte kudasai. Please wait for about five minutes.

3. The postposition *ni* follows a number that refers to the time at which something takes place. This postposition is equivalent to 'at' or 'in' in English.

sanji ni	at 3 o'clock
getsuyōbi ni	on Monday
nigatsu ni	in February

4. Note the use of *yo, shichi* and *ku* in the following:

ichiji	one o'clock		*shichiji*	seven o'clock
niji	two	„	*hachiji*	eight	„
sanji	three	„	*kuji*	nine	„
yoji	four	„	*jūji*	ten	„
goji	five	„	*jūichiji*	eleven	„
rokuji	six	„	*jūniji*	twelve	„

D

Itsu desu ka?	When?
Dōshite desu ka?	Why?
Dō iu imi desu ka?	What does it mean?

LESSON XXI

A

naniyō (óo) bi what day of the week
getsuyō (óo) bi Monday
doyō (óo) bi Saturday
kimásu (kuru) come
maishū every week
kinyō (óo) bi Friday
sakana fish
áru certain; some
nichiyō (óo) bi Sunday
déshita was
ashita tomorrow
suiyō (óo) bi Wednesday
mokuyō (óo) bi Thursday
kayō (óo) bi Tuesday
kyōkai church

Kurisúmasu Christmas
nishū (úu) kan two weeks
yasumimásu, (yasumu) take vacation
benkyō-shimásu (benkyō-suru) study
ototoi day before yesterday
warúi bad
ténki weather
áme rain
kara from
yūgata early evening
máde till
furimásu (furu) fall
asátte day after tomorrow

B

Kyō wa naniyōbi desu ka?

Getsuyōbi desu.
Anata wa doyōbi ni gakkō e kimasu ka?
Kanadajin wa maishū kinyōbi ni sakana o tabemasu ka?
Hai, aru hito wa tabemasu.

Kinō wa nichiyōbi deshita ka?
Hai, nichiyōbi deshita.
Ashita wa suiyōbi desu ka, mokuyōbi desu ka?
Suiyōbi demo mokuyōbi demo arimasen. Kayōbi desu.
Anata wa nichiyōbi ni kyōkai e ikimasu ka?
Watakushitachi wa Kurisumasu ni nishūkan yasumimasu.
Maishū nanjikan Nihongo o benkyō-shimasu ka?
Maishū gojikan benkyō-shimasu.

Ototoi wa warui tenki deshita ne.
Ame ga asa kara yūgata made furimashita.
Watakushi wa asatte Shiatoru e ikimasu.

C

1. The days of the week are derived from the following seven elements of the universe.

nichiyōbi	sun
getsuyōbi	moon
kayōbi	fire
suiyōbi	water
mokuyōbi	tree
kinyōbi	metal
doyōbi	earth

Bi of '*-yōbi*' is sometimes dropped.

2. The past tense of *desu* is *deshita*.

3 The construction pattern ...*demo* ...*demo arimasen* corresponds to '...is neither ...nor' in English.

Nihonjin demo Kanadajin He is neither a Japanese nor
demo arimasen. a Canadian.

Atsukumo samukumo ari-masen.	It is neither hot nor cold.
Eigo mo Nihongo mo hana-shimasu.	He speaks both English and Japanese.

4. The Japanese present tense expresses futurity.

Ashita ikimasu.	I will go tomorrow.

5. *Shūkan* is used in counting the number of weeks.

isshūkan	one week	*rokushūkan*	six weeks
nishūkan	two weeks	*nanashūkan*	seven weeks
sanshūkan	three weeks	*hasshūkan*	eight weeks
yonshūkan	four weeks	*kyūshūkan*	nine weeks
goshūkan	five weeks	*jisshūkan*	ten weeks

D

Dō shimashita ka?	What happened?
Dōzo odaiji ni.	Take care of yourself.
Dōzo okamai naku.	Don't go to any trouble on my account.

LESSON XXII

A

sángatsu	March	*jūichigatsu*	November
shigatsu	April	*áki*	autumn
gógatsu	May	*jūnigatsu*	December
háru	spring	*ichigatsu*	January
rokugatsu	June	*nigatsu*	February
shichigatsu	July	*fuyú*	winter
hachigatsu	August	*atatakái*	warm
natsú	summer	*suzushíi*	cool
kúgatsu	September	*sakura*	cherryblossoms
jūgatsu	October	*nángatsu*	what month

saku bloom
deshō(óo) will
owari end
hajime beginning
yukí snow
nakagoro about the middle
rainen next year
kotoshi this year
nánnen what year
sén thousand
kyū(úu)*hyaku* 900

kyónen last year
imásu (*iru*) stay; exist
kongetsu this month
ráigetsu next month
séngetsu last month
nánnen how many years
yonen four years
nankágetsu how many months
nikágetsu two months

B

Sangatsu, shigatsu, gogatsu wa haru de, rokugatsu, shichigatsu, hachigatsu wa natsu desu.
Kugatsu, jūgatsu, jūichigatsu wa aki de, jūnigatsu, ichigatsu,
nigatsu wa fuyu desu.

Haru wa atatakakute, natsu wa atsui desu.
Aki wa suzushikute, fuyu wa samui desu.

Sakura wa nangatsu ni saku deshō ka?
Sangatsu no owari ka shigatsu no hajime ni sakimasu.

Yuki wa nangatsu ni furimasu ka?
Jūnigatsu no nakagoro ni furu deshō.
Ame wa nigatsu ni furu deshō ka?
Iie, furanai deshō.

Anata wa rainen Tōkyō e ikimasu ka?
Kotoshi wa nannen desu ka?
Sen kyūhyaku rokujūsan-nen desu.
Buraun-san wa kyonen Bankūbā ni imashita ka?
Iie, imasen deshita.

Kongetsu wa nangatsu desu ka?
Jūgatsu desu.

Dewa, raigetsu wa jūichigatsu desu ne.
Sengetsu wa kugatsu deshita.

Gakusei wa daigaku de nannen benkyō-shimasu ka?
Yonen benkyō-shimasu.
Anatagata wa nankagetsu Nihongo o naratte imasu ka?
Nikagetsu gurai naratte imasu.

C

1. The te-form of the adjective and the verb was dealt with before:

Bangohan o tabete, ikimashita.	I ate supper and went.
Kono heya wa ōkikute, kirei desu ne.	This room is large and clean, isn't it?
Anzen de hayai n desu.	It is safe and fast.
Samukute ikimasen deshita.	It was cold; so I did not go.

As the above sentence indicates, the te-form sometimes signifies the reason or cause.

The following phrases should be easy to form:

akakute chiisai hako	a red and small box
yasukute ii enpitsu	a cheap and fine pencil

2. Deshō which is the conjectural form of desu is equivalent to 'perhaps' or 'I think' in English.

Samui deshō.	Perhaps it is cold.
Yomu deshō.	I think he will read it.

In the above sentence containing the verb yomu, the polite form yomimasu can be used in very polite speech.

3. As was mentioned before, the negative form of masu is masen. There is another way of forming the negative. It is called the plain or non-polite style.

(a) Group I Verbs

Dictionary form	Negative form
kiku (hear)	*kika-nai*
yasumu (rest)	*yasuma-nai*
narau (learn)	*narawa-nai*
hanasu (speak)	*hanasa-nai*
motsu (hold)	*mota-nai*
nugu (undress)	*nuga-nai*
yobu (call)	*yoba-nai*
shinu (die)	*shina-nai*
toru (take)	*tora-nai*
kaeru (go back)	*kaera-nai*
hairu (enter)	*haira-nai*

As is seen above, the final *u* must be replaced by *a* (1st base) followed by *nai*. The final *u* preceded by another vowel (*a*, *i*, *u*, or *o*) is changed into *wa*.

(b) Group II Verbs

taberu (eat)	*tabe-nai*
miru (look)	*mi-nai*

The final syllable *ru* should be dropped and *nai* should be added.

(c) Irregular Verbs

kuru (come)	*ko-nai*
suru (do)	*shi-nai*

(d) True Adjectives

ōkii (large)	*ōkiku-nai*
samui (cold)	*samuku-nai*

(e) Quasi-adjectives

kirei-na (pretty)	*kirei ja (de) nai*
shizuka-na (quiet)	*shizuka ja (de) nai*

The polite form of the above can be used in very polite speech:

Plain style	Polite style
Hanasanai deshō.	*Hanashimasen deshō.*
Tabenai deshō.	*Tabemasen deshō.*

4. *Mashō,* which is the conjectural form of *masu,* is generally used for the 1st person. It is also employed in inviting the 2nd person to cooperate with the 1st person. Unlike *deshō, mashō* expresses a decision.

Watakushi ga ikimashō.   I will go.

Issho-ni tabemashō ka?   Let's eat together, shall we?

5. There are three styles of conversation in the Japanese language: the plain style, the normal polite style, and the honorific style.

The plain style, which is used among family members, close friends, and in talking to a social inferior, is too rude.

The honorific style, which is used when politeness and respect should be shown towards a superior, is too ceremonious.

The normal polite style is half way between the above two styles and can be used by both men and women. In this style, a sentence must end in the polite style, but verbs and adjectives in the middle of a sentence may be in the plain style.

6. The number of months is counted as follows:

ikkagetsu (hitotsuki)	*gokagetsu* five months
one month	*rokkagetsu* six months
nikagetsu (futatsuki)	*nanakagetsu* seven months
two months	*hachikagetsu* eight months
sankagetsu (mitsuki)	*kyūkagetsu* nine months
three months	*jikkagetsu* ten months
yonkagetsu (yotsuki) four months	

D

Kashikomarimashita.	Certainly, sir (madam).
	With pleasure.
Dōzo osaki ni.	After you, sir (madam).
Omatase shimashita.	Sorry to have kept you waiting.
Oisogi desu ka?	Are you in a hurry?

LESSON XXIII

A

nánnichi what day of the month	*misé* shop
mikká 3rd	*maigetsu* every month
itsuka 5th	*jū (úu) gonichi* 15th
chigaimásu (*chigau*) be wrong; differ	*tanjō (óo) bi* birthday
yokká 4th	*jūichinichi* 11th
futsuka 2nd	*ítsu ... ka?* when ...?
tsuitachi 1st	*nijūgónichi* 25th

B

Kyō wa nannichi desu ka?
Mikka desu.
Dewa, ashita wa itsuka desu ne.
Iie, chigaimasu. Ashita wa yokka desu.
Ototoi wa futsuka deshita ka?
Iie, tsuitachi deshita.

Tōkyō no aru mise wa maigetsu tsuitachi to jūgonichi ni yasumimasu.

Anata no tanjōbi wa itsu desu ka?
Nigatsu jūichinichi desu.
Kurisumasu wa itsu desu ka?
Jūnigatsu nijūgonichi desu.

C

1. Note the following irregularity:

tsuitachi	1st	*itsuka*	5th
futsuka	2nd	*muika*	6th
mikka	3rd	*nanoka*	7th
yokka	4th	*yōka*	8th

kokonoka	9th	nijūichinichi	21st
tōka	10th	nijūninichi	22nd
jūichinichi	11th	nijūsannichi	23rd
jūninichi	12th	nijūyokka	24th
jūsannichi	13th	nijūgonichi	25th
jūyokka	14th	nijūrokunichi	26th
jūgonichi	15th	nijūshichinichi	27th
jūrokunichi	16th	nijūhachinichi	28th
jūshichinichi	17th	nijūkunichi	29th
jūhachinichi	18th	sanjūnichi	30th
jūkunichi	19th	sanjūichinichi	31st
hatsuka	20th		

2. The word *tsuitachi* is used only in the sense of the first day of the month. Don't confuse it with the word *ichinichi*, which means 'a day'.

Tsuitachi ni kimashita.	I came on the 1st.
Ichinichi yasumimashita.	I took a day off.
Mikka ni ikimasu.	I will go on the 3rd.
Mikka yasumimasu.	I will take three days off.

D

Sō kamo shiremasen.	Maybe so.
Kochira wa K-san desu.	Allow me to present Mr. K.
Hajimemashite.	How do you do?
	Glad to meet you.
K to mōshimasu.	My name is K.

LESSON XXIV

A

átsuku narimásu (naru) become hot	naránai do not become
akaruku náru become bright	uisuki whisky
kuraku náru become dark	... to whenever; if; when

kaó face
akaku náru become red
chittómo not a bit (followed
by neg.)
jōzu ni náru become good
... *to* that
omoimásu (*omou*) think
sámuku náru become cold
kaze wind

fúku blow
hokori dust
tátsu arise
arau wash
kírei ni náru become clean;
become pretty
jōbu ni náru b e c o m e
healthy; become strong

B

Bankūbā wa itsu atsuku narimasu ka?
Shichigatsu ni sukoshi atsuku narimasu.
Asa nanji goro akaruku narimasu ka?
Goji goro akaruku narimasu.
Yūgata rokuji ni kuraku naru deshō ka?
Iie, kuraku naranai deshō.

Uisukī o nomu to, kao ga akaku narimasu ka?
Iie, chittomo akaku narimasen.

Mainichi hanasu to, jōzu ni narimasu ka?
Jōzu ni naru to omoimasu.

Nihongo wa muzukashii to omoimasu ka?
Ame ga furu to, samuku narimasu ka, atsuku narimasu ka?
Ame ga furu to, samuku narimasu.
Kaze ga fuku to, hokori ga tachimasu.

Kono hankachi o arau to, kirei ni naru to omoimasu ka?
Kirei ni naranai to omoimasu.
Aruku to, jōbu ni narimasu nē.

C

1. The verb *naru* meaning 'become' or 'change into' is used with
the adverbial form of a true adjective and a quasi-adjective.

Atsuku narimashita.   It has become hot.

Jōzu ni narimashita.   He became good at it.

2. The postposition *to* placed at the end of a non-final clause corresponds to 'whenever', 'when' or 'if' and is always used after the present tense form, even when the verb of the final clause is in the past tense. *To* is seldom used with the imperative form.

Ame ga furu to, samuku nari-   Whenever it rains, it be-
masu.   comes cold.
Gakkō ga owaru to, uchi e   When school was over,
kaerimashita.   they went home.

3. The English conjunction 'that' is expressed by *to* in Japanese.

Takai to omoimasu ka?   Do you think that it is ex-
    pensive?
Omoshiroi to iimashita.   He said that it was interest-
    ing.
Kuru to kikimashita.   I heard that you would come.

D

Omedetō gozaimasu.   Congratulations!
Shinnen omedetō gozaimasu.   Happy New Year!
K-san o onegai shimasu.   Mr. K, please.
K-san irasshaimasu ka?   I'd like to talk to Mr. K.

LESSON XXV

A

shūmatsu week-end   *gógo* p.m.; afternoon
dókoka somewhere   *éiga* movie
ikitái wish to go   *mítaku arimasén* do not
ongákukai concert   wish to see
ongaku music   *kutabiréru* get tired

nódo throat
kawáku become dry
nánika something
onaka stomach
suku become empty
... *tokí ni* when

irimásu (iru) need
fūtō envelope
kukkī cookies
tsukúru make
batā butter
issho-ni together

B

Shūmatsu ni dokoka e ikitai desu ka?
Ongakukai e ikitai desu. Ii, ongaku o kikitai desu kara.
Kyō no gogo eiga o mitai desu ka?
Iie, mitaku arimasen. Kutabiremashita kara.
Ima kōhī o nomitai desu ka?
Hai, nomitai desu. Nodo ga kawakimashita kara.
Nanika tabetai desu ka?
Iie, nannimo tabetaku arimasen. Onaka ga suite imasen.

Tegami o kakitai toki ni, nani ga irimasu ka?
Kami to fūtō to pen ga irimasu.
Kukkī o tsukuritai toki ni, batā ga irimasu ka?

Kinō issho-ni ikitai deshita ka?
Iie, ikitaku arimasen deshita.

C

1. *Tai*, which is a desiderative, expresses a desire to do something. It is attached to the second base and is equivalent to 'wish to ...' in English.

(a) Group I Verbs

2nd base	Tai-form
kiki-masu (hear)	*kiki-tai*
yasumi-masu (rest)	*yasumi-tai*
narai-masu (learn)	*narai-tai*
hanashi-masu (speak)	*hanashi-tai*
mochi-masu (hold)	*mochi-tai*

2nd base	*Tai*-form
nugi-masu (undress)	*nugi-tai*
yobi-masu (call)	*yobi-tai*
shini-masu (die)	*shini-tai*
tori-masu (take)	*tori-tai*
kaeri-masu (go back)	*kaeri-tai*
hairi-masu (enter)	*hairi-tai*

(b) Group II Verbs

tabe-masu (eat)	*tabe-tai*
mi-masu (look)	*mi-tai*

(c) Irregular Verbs

ki-masu (come)	*ki-tai*
shi-masu (do)	*shi-tai*

Tōkyō e ikitai desu ka?	Do you want to go to Tokyo?
Tabetaku arimasen.	I do not want to eat.

2. (a) *Mizu o nomitai desu.*

   (b) *Mizu ga nomitai desu.*

The above two constructions are possible. In (a) the speaker's mind is on the verb *nomu*, with the result that he uses *o*, whereas in (b) his mind is on the adjective-like auxiliary *tai* which conjugates like a true adjective, thus using *ga*. In other words, the postposition *o* and *ga* are interchangeable in these constructions.

3. The expression ...*toki ni* (or *toki wa*) corresponds to English 'when', and is preceded by either the present tense or the past tense. It refers to a particular point or period of time.

Taberu toki ni tsukaimasu.	When I eat, I use it.
Katta toki ni ii deshita.	When I bought it, it was good.

4. The verb *iru* meaning 'need' or 'be necessary' is an intransitive verb in Japanese. Hence it demands *ga* or *wa* instead

of *o*.

>*Okane ga irimasu ka?*   Do you need any money?

5. The following words take *ga* or *wa*: *hoshii* (desirous), *suki*
(fond), *kirai* (dislike), *dekiru* (possible), *kowai* (afraid), *aru*
(own), *wakaru* (understand), etc.

D

Shibaraku desu ne.	I've not seen you for ages.
Zannen desu ne.	What a pity!
Oki no doku desu.	I feel sorry for you.
	That's too bad.
Odekake desu ka?	Are you going out?

LESSON XXVI

A

hanásu kotó ga dekimásu (*de-kiru*) be able to speak

...*ka dō (óo) ka* whether or not

shirú know

ichijíkan de in an hour

hetá desu be poor; not skilful

hanasemásu (*hanaseru*) be able to speak

kanji Chinese characters

mō sukóshi a little more

pán bread

taberaremásu (*taberareru*) be able to eat

katái hard

gaitō overcoat

kiraremásu (*kirareru*) be able to wear

B

Anata wa Eigo o hanasu koto ga dekimasu ka?
Hai, dekimasu.
Gurīku-san wa Nihongo o hanasu koto ga dekimasu ka?
Iie, dekimasen.
Ano kata wa Nihon no shinbun o yomu koto ga dekimasu ka?
Dekiru ka dō ka shirimasen.
Bikutoria e ichijikan de iku koto ga dekimasu ka?

Iie, dekinai deshō.
Ohashi de taberu koto ga dekimasu ka?
Hai, heta desu ga, dekimasu.

Anata wa Supeingo ga hanasemasu ka?
Hai, sukoshi hanasemasu.
Jōnzu-san wa 'kanji' ga kakemasu ka?
Kakeru to omoimasu.
Mō sukoshi hayaku arukemasen ka?
Iie, arukemasu.
Kono pan wa taberaremasu ka?
Iie, katakute taberaremasen.
Sono gaitō wa chiisakute, kiraremasen.

C

1. Potentiality is expressed by attaching the dictionary form of any verbs to the pattern *koto ga dekiru*.

Kau koto ga dekimasu.	We can buy it.
Taberu koto ga dekimasen.	You cannot eat it.
Iku koto ga dekimashita ka?	Could you go?

Koto ga dekiru literally means 'a fact is possible'.

Eigo ga dekimasu ka?	Do you speak English?
	(Lit. Is English possible?)

2. The pattern ...*ka dō ka* corresponds to English 'whether or not'.

Ii ka dō ka shirimasen.	I do not know whether it is good or not.
Kuru ka dō ka kiite kudasai.	Please ask him whether he will come or not.

3. The postposition *de* is used in reference to the time required.

Nisanpun de owarimasu.	It will be over in two or three minutes.

4. There is another way of expressing potentiality. This shorter form is more common in ordinary conversation.

(a) Group I Verbs

Dictionary form	Potential form
kiku (hear)	*kikeru*
yasumu (rest)	*yasumeru*
hanasu (speak)	*hanaseru*
motsu (hold)	*moteru*
nugu (undress)	*nugeru*
yobu (call)	*yoberu*
shinu (die)	*shineru*
toru (take)	*toreru*
kaeru (go back)	*kaereru*
hairu (enter)	*haireru*
kau (buy)	*kaeru*

The final *u* of the dictionary form is replaced by *eru*.

(b) Group II Verbs

taberu (eat)	*taberareru*
kiru (wear)	*kirareru*

The final *ru* of the dictionary form is replaced by *rareru*.

(c) Irregular Verbs

kuru	*korareru*

The shorter potential form of the irregular verb *suru* is rarely used; the expression *dekiru* is used as the shorter potential form corresponding to *suru*. Thus '*benkyō-suru koto ga dekiru*' is shortened to '*benkyō dekiru*'.

Another important point about these shorter potential verbs is that they take *ga* or *wa* instead of *o*.

Anata wa Nihongo ga hanasemasu ne.
You can speak Japanese, can't you?
Kore wa ōkikute taberaremasen.
This is so big I cannot eat.

D

Abunai!	Look out!
Yatte mimashō.	I'll try.
Muri desu.	That's impossible.
Ano ne.	Listen!

LESSON XXVII

A

kitá (kimashita) came	*pāti* party
tátte iru (imasu) be standing	*futótte iru (futoru)* stout
áru (arimasu) exist; is	*tábun* maybe
to iu (iimasu) call	*shikáshi* however
tsukau use	*yasete iru (yaseru)* thin
sei make	*sō(óo) desu* they say; I hear
míta (mimashita) saw	*háreta (hareru)* clear; fine
dō(óo) how	*kumótta (kumoru)* cloudy
totemo very	*gorufu* golfing
dáre who	*ni* for
furúi old	*tótta (toru)* took
yogoreta soiled	*shashin* photograph
waishatsu shirt	*miséru* show
	hi day

B

Kinō kita tegami
Kodomo ga yomu hon
Soko ni tatte iru hito

Tsukue no ue ni aru hon wa donata no desu ka?
Tsukue no ue ni aru hon wa watakushi no desu.
Takami-san ga yonde iru shinbun wa nan to iu namae desu ka?
'Asahi' to iu namae desu.
Anata ga tsukatte iru mannenhitsu wa Kanada sei desu ka?
Hai, sō desu.

Senshū mita eiga wa dō deshita ka?

Totemo ii deshita.

Asuko ni iru hito wa dare desu ka?

Asuko ni iru hito wa watakushi no furui tomodachi de, Kūpā to iu hito desu.

Yogoreta waishatsu o kite, pātī e ikitai desu ka?

Iie, ikitaku arimasen.

Futotte iru hito wa natsu atsui desu ka?

Tabun atsui deshō. Shikashi, yasete iru hito wa fuyu samui sō desu.

Hareta hi to kumotta hi to, dotchi ga gorufu ni ii desu ka?

Hareta hi no hō ga ii desu.

Anata no totta shashin o misete kudasai.

C

1. There are no relative pronouns in Japanese. A relative clause ending with a verb or an adjective in the plain present or past tense is placed before a noun as a modifier. However, the final clause must end in the polite style.

kinō kita tegami	a letter which came yesterday (Lit. yesterday came letter)
ōkikatta uchi	a house that was large
akakunai hon	a book which is not red
yasukunakatta kuruma	a car which was not cheap
megane o kakete inai hito	a person who is not wearing glasses
kodomo ga yomu hon	books which children read
soko ni tatte iru hito	a person who is standing there
shinbun o yonde ita Nihonjin	a Japanese who was reading a newspaper
kiite inakatta gakusei	students who were not listening
kōhī o nomanai hito	people who do not drink coffee

shiranakatta kotoba	the word which I did not know
Eigo ga hanaseru K-san	Mr. K who can speak English
namae ga kakenai hito	people who cannot write their names
yomete kakeru hito	a person who can read and write
A-san ga hataraite iru kaisha	the firm where Mr. A is employed
anata no tomatta hoteru	the hotel into which you checked

2. How verbs are converted from the plain present to the plain past is shown below:

(a) Group I Verbs

Plain present	Plain past
kiku (hear)	*kiita*
yasumu (rest)	*yasunda*
narau (learn)	*naratta*
hanasu (speak)	*hanashita*
motsu (hold)	*motta*
nugu (undress)	*nuida*
yobu (call)	*yonda*
shinu (die)	*shinda*
toru (take)	*totta*
kaeru (go back)	*kaetta*
hairu (enter)	*haitta*
iku (go)	*itta*

(b) Group II Verbs

taberu (eat)	*tabeta*
miru (look)	*mita*

(c) Irregular Verbs

kuru (come)	*kita*
suru (do)	*shita*

The above indicates that the plain past can be formed by replacing the final *e* of *te*-form by *a*.

(a) Group I Verbs

Plain present (negative)	Plain past (negative)
kika-nai (do not hear)	*kika-nakatta*
yasuma-nai (dot not rest)	*yasuma-nakatta*
narawa-nai (do not learn)	*narawa-nakatta*
hanasa-nai (do not speak)	*hanasa-nakatta*
mota-nai (do not hold)	*mota-nakatta*
nuga-nai (do not undress)	*nuga-nakatta*
yoba-nai (do not call)	*yoba-nakatta*
shina-nai (do not die)	*shina-nakatta*
tora-nai (do not take)	*tora-nakatta*
kaera-nai (do not go back)	*kaera-nakatta*
haira-nai (do not enter)	*haira-nakatta*

(b) Group II Verbs

tabe-nai (do not eat)	*tabe-nakatta*
mi-nai (dot not look)	*mi-nakatta*

(c) Irregular Verbs

ko-nai (do not come)	*ko-nakatta*
shi-nai (do not do)	*shi-nakatta*

As is seen in the above, the adjective-like auxiliary *nai* is replaced by *nakatta*.

The plain past form of the present progressive form *-te iru* is *-te ita*.

3. The conversion of the adjective from the plain present into

the plain past is as follows:

Plain present	Plain past
samui (cold)	*samukatta*
takai (high)	*takakatta*
warui (bad)	*warukatta*

, As the above indicates, the final *i* is replaced by *katta*.

Plain present (negative)	Plain past (negative)
samuku-nai (is not cold)	*samuku-nakatta*
takaku-nai (is not high)	*takaku-nakatta*
waruku-nai (is not bad)	*waruku-nakatta*

The copula *desu,* which is a kind of equal sign, is *da* in the plain present form. The plain past of this *da* is *datta.*

The copula *ja arimasen* is changed to *ja nai* in the plain present form, of which past form is *ja nakatta.*

shichō de aru Ōyama-san	Mr. Ōyama who is the mayor
sensei datta Eikokujin	An Englishman who was a teacher
tomodachi ja nai hito	a man who is not a friend of mine
shizuka ja nakatta machi	a town which was not quiet

4. (a) *watakushi ga iku tokoro*   the place where I go
    (b) *watakushi no iku tokoro*   „

The above two constructions are possible. There is no difference in meaning. The postposition *ga* in a modifying clause can be replaced by *no.*

5.   English past participles are used as noun modifiers such as 'broken chair', 'soft boiled egg', etc. Likewise Japanese verbs meaning 'grow so-and-so' or 'become so-and-so' are used as noun modifiers in the plain past form.

futotta hito	a stout man
futotte iru hito	„

yaseta hito	a thin man
yasete iru hito	„

kumotta hi	a cloudy day
kumotte iru hi	„

hareta hi	a clear day
harete iru hi	„

yogoreta hankachi	a soiled handkerchief
yogorete iru hankachi	„

When used predicatively, only the progressive form is to be employed:

Kyō wa kumotte imasu.	It's cloudy today.
Kinō wa harete imashita.	It was fine yesterday.
Futotte imasen.	He is not stout.
Yasete imasu ka?	Is he thin?
Yogorete imasu nē.	It's dirty, isn't it?

6. In addition to the true adjectives which end in *i*, the quasi-adjectives which end in *na*, and the above-mentioned participle-like verbs, there are modifiers which are formed by nouns plus *no*.

kin no tokei	a gold watch
iroiro-no mono	various things
hontō-no hanashi	a true story
futsū-no kangae	an ordinary idea

These quasi-adjectives ending in *na* and *no* are similar in usage:

(a) *Sore wa hontō-no hanashi desu.*   That is a true story.
(b) *Sono hanashi wa hontō desu.*   The story is true.

7. Some nouns may take either *na* or *no*:

iroiro-na; iroiro-no	various
tokubetsu-na; tokubetsu-no	special

atarimae-na; atarimae-no   reasonable

Caution must be exercised about some *ai*-ending quasi-adjectives:

aimai-na	ambiguous	*kirai-na*	disgusting
hantai-no	opposite	*saiwai-na*	lucky
igai-na	unexpected	*yakkai-na*	bothersome

8. The expression *to iu* means 'called' or 'named'.

Yamada to iu Nihonjin	A Japanese called Yamada
'Painful' wa Nihongo de nan to iimasu ka.?	What is the Japanese for 'painful'?

9. A polite request is expressed by *-te kudasai*.

Ashita kite kudasai.	Please come tomorrow.
Mizu o kudasai.	Give me a glass of water, please.

Nasai after the 2nd base of the verb expresses command.

Kaki nasai.	Write it.
Tabe nasai.	Eat it.

10. The pattern *sō desu*, which corresponds to 'I hear' or 'they say' in English, follows the plain form of verbs and adjectives. It is placed at the end of a sentence.

Ii sō desu.	I hear it is good.
Kau sō desu.	He will buy it, I hear.
Samukatta sō desu.	It was cold, I understand.
Takakunai sō desu.	It is not high, I hear.

D

Sore wa sō to. Toki ni.	By the way. Incidentally.
Sore de omoidashimashita ga.	That reminds me.

Ēto. Sō desu nē.   Let me see. Well.

LESSON XXVIII

A

nánte ... deshō(óo)! How   *sūpu* soup
  ...!   *karái* salty
kawaíi cute   *ki* tree

B

Nante kawaii deshō.!
Kono sūpu wa nante karai deshō!
Kinō wa nante samukatta deshō!
Nante ōkiku natta deshō!
Nante kirei ni natta deshō!
Nante kirei-na hana deshō!
Nante takai ki deshō!

C

1. Exclamatory feeling is expressed by the pattern *nante ...(n) deshō!*, which is equivalent to 'How ..!' or 'What ...!' in English.

2. The pattern *nan to iu* followed by a noun can also be used to express exclamatory feeling.

   Nan to iu ii tenki deshō!   What a fine day!

D

Dō omoimasu ka?   What do you think?
Sono tōri desu.   That's right.
Machigaemashita.   I'm wrong.
Onegai ga arimasu.   I have a favor to ask of you.
Kono sētā o kite   Try this sweater on.
  goran nasai.

LESSON XXIX

A

bín bottle	*ehágaki* picture postcard
yoko side	*kitté* postage stamp
káite áru be written	*harú* paste; affix
ireru put in	*kabé* wall
matchi matches	*kakéru* hang
okú put; place	*e* picture
yuká floor	

B

Bin no yoko ni nani ga kaite arimasu ka?
Eigo to Nihongo ga kaite arimasu.
Kono chiisana hako no naka ni nani ga irete arimasu ka?
Matchi ga irete arimasu.
Anata no ōkina kaban wa doko ni oite arimasu ka?
Yuka no ue ni oite arimasu.

Doa wa akete arimasu ka, shimete arimasu ka?
Ehagaki ni kitte ga hatte arimasu ka?
Iie, hatte arimasen.

Kabe ni nani ga kakete arimasu ka?
E ga kakete arimasu.

C

1. The *te*-form plus *iru* was dealt with before. The *te*-form plus *aru*, which denotes a state or condition resulting from somebody's action, is used only with transitive verbs. Note the postposition *ga* or *wa*.

   Mado ga shimete arimasu.   The window is closed.
   Mado o shimete imasu.   I am closing the window.

2.   (a)   *Gaitō ga kiete imasu.*   (*kieru*, go out)

(b)   *Gaitō ga keshite arimasu.*   (*kesu,* put out)

The English equivalent of the above two sentences will be 'the outdoor lamp is out'. However, (a) indicates that the outdoor lamp has gone out naturally, or that it has been intentionally put out by somebody, whereas (b) indicates that the outdoor lamp has been put out by somebody.

3.   *Chiisana* and *ōkina* are similar in meaning to *chiisai* and *ōkii* respectively. There are some such modifiers in Japanese. Note that they are not used predicatively.

> *Kono ōkina jisho wa watakushi no desu.*
> This big dictionary is mine.
>
> *Kono jisho wa ōkii desu nē.*
> This dictionary is big, isn't it?

4.   Besides the above, the following are in common use:

atataka-na warm	*masshiro-na* snow-white
komaka-na minute; fine	*okashi-na* strange; funny
makkuro-na jet-black	*yawaraka-na* soft

D

Nanika goyō desu ka?	What can I do for you?
Naruhodo.	I see.
Dotchi demo ii desu.	It makes no difference.
Onegai shimasu.	I entreat you.

LESSON XXX

A

akete mo ii may open	*arukinágara* while walking
káite wa ikemasén (*ikenai*) must not write	*núide mo ii* may take off
kyōshitsu class-room	*osake* Japanese wine

unten-suru drive   kámo shiremasén (shire-
abunai dangerous   nai) may (possibility)

B

. Mado o akete mo ii desu ka?
Hai, akete mo ii desu.
Enpitsu de tegami o kaite mo ii desu ka?
Iie, kaite wa ikemasen.
Kyōshitsu de bīru o nonde mo ii desu ka?
Iie, nonde wa ikemasen.

Arukinagara ringo o tabete mo ii desu ka?
Iie, arukinagara ringo o tabete wa ikemasen.
Uwagi o nuide mo ii desu ka?
Hai, nuide mo ii desu.
Osake o nonde jidōsha o unten-shite wa ikemasen ka?
Hai, unten-shite wa ikemasen. Abunai kamo shiremasen.

C

1. The te-form plus mo ii denotes permission. The pattern
literally means 'is good even …ing', hence 'all right even
if …'. It corresponds to 'may'.

    Haitte mo ii desu ka?   May I come in?

2. The pattern te wa ikenai is equivalent to 'must not' in English. This expression literally means 'won't do if …ing'.

    Enpitsu de kaite wa ikemasen. You must not write in pencil.

3. The expression nagara is tacked on to the 2nd base of a
verb. It is equivalent to 'while' in English. Note that the
two actions are performed simultaneously by the same person
or persons.

    Ocha o nominagara Yamada-san to hanashimashita.
        I talked with Mr. Yamada over tea.

4. *O* of the word *ocha* is an honorific prefix. It is used before a great number of nouns. The honorific idea is at times vague, as in the word *ocha*; and at other times it is clear, as in the word *otegami* meaning 'your letter'.

Go is another honorific prefix in common use. It generally is placed before those nouns which are of Chinese origin; *goryokō* (your trip), *goshinsetsu* (your kindness), etc.

5. *Kamo shirenai* is the equivalent of English 'may' or 'may be'. It is preceded by the present and past tense of verbs and adjectives in the plain form. It can also be used with a noun or a quasi-adjective.

Anmari kurai kamo shiremasen.	It may be too dark.
Ame ga furu kamo shiremasen.	It may rain.
Motto takakatta kamo shiremasen.	It may have been more expensive.
Sō itta kamo shiremasen.	I may have said so.
Eikokujin kamo shiremasen.	He may be an Englishman.
Takakunai kamo shiremasen.	It may not be expensive.
Yomanakatta kamo shirenai n desu.	He may not have read it.
Kakeru kamo shiremasen.	I may be able to write it.

LESSON XXXI

A

kusuri medicine
nómeba (*nomu*)
　　if one drinks (takes)
byōki sickness; disease
naóru get well

yukkúri slowly
nemuku náru
　　become sleepy
dásu mail; put out
ni to; in

tsúku arrive
tsumori désu intend
ma ni áu catch; be in time
mochíron of course
okane money
nákereba (nai) if one has
  no; if there is not
háiru enter
miéru be visible

kikoeru be audible
ikanáide kudasái
  please do not go
tōi far
kuruma car
iku hō(óo) ga íi
  had better go
kirai nára if one dislikes
jōbu-na strong
kau buy

B

Kusuri o nomeba, byōki wa naorimasu ka?
Hai, taitei naorimasu.
Yukkuri hanaseba, wakarimasu ka?
Hai, wakarimasu.
Takusan tabereba, nemuku narimasu ka?
Hai, tokidoki nemuku narimasu.
Kyō kono tegami o daseba, asatte Otawa ni tsukimasu ka?
Hai, tsuku deshō.

Ame ga fureba, uchi ni imasu ka?
Hai, iru tsumori desu.
Ima ikeba, sanji no basu ni ma ni aimasu ka?
Hai, ma ni aimasu.
Yoku benkyō-sureba, jōzu ni naremasu ka?
Hai, mochiron jōzu ni naremasu yo.

Yasukereba, kaitai desu ka?
Hai, kaitai desu.
Atsukereba, dō shimasu ka?
Atsukereba, mado ya doa o akemasu.
Okane ga nakereba, hairemasen ka?
Hai, hairemasen.

Akarukereba, miemasu ga, kurakereba, miemasen.
Chikakereba, kikoemasu ga, tōkereba, kikoemasen.

Tenki ga warukereba, ikanaide kudasai.
Tōkereba, kuruma ka basu de iku hō ga ii deshō.
Kirai nara, tabenaide kudasai.
Jōbu nara, kusuri wa irimasen.

C

1. The provisional form meaning 'if so-and-so happens' or 'if so-and-so is the case' is made in the following way:

(a) Group I Verbs

Dictionary form	Provisional form
yomu (read)	*yomeba*
hanasu (speak)	*hanaseba*
kaku (write)	*kakeba*

(b) Group II Verbs

taberu (eat)	*tabereba*
miru (look)	*mireba*

(c) Irregular Verbs

suru (do)	*sureba*
kuru (come)	*kureba*

As the above indicates, the final *u* of verbs is replaced by *eba*.

Adjectives

takai (high)	*takakereba*
ōkii (big)	*ōkikereba*
nai (non-existent)	*nakereba*

The above shows that the final *i* of true adjectives must be replaced by *kereba*.

This construction cannot be used with quasi-adjectives.

The following negative forms are easy to make:

Plain form	Provisional form
yomanai (do not read)	*yomanakereba*
tabenai (do not eat)	*tabenakereba*
yasukunai (not cheap)	*yasukunakereba*
jōzu ja nai (n o t g o o d ; poor)	*jōzu ja nakereba*

The provisional usually refers to the present or the future.

2. The particle *ni* denotes a point; *e* a direction.

Bankūbā ni goji ni tsuki-mashita.	I got to Vancouver at 5.
Nihon e rainen ikimasu.	I'll go to Japan next year.

3. The verb *ma ni au* demands *ni*.

Kisha ni ma ni aimasen deshita.	I could not make the train.

4. Intention is expressed by the word *tsumori*.

Iku tsumori desu.	He intends to go.
Kau tsumori deshita.	I intended to buy it.
Sō suru tsumori ja arima-sen.	I do not intend to do so.

5. *Yo* placed at the end of a sentence means 'I assure you' or 'I tell you'.

6. *Mieru* (be visible) and *kikoeru* (be audible) are intransitive verbs and take *ga* or *wa*. Compare these two verbs with *miru* (see) and *kiku* (hear) which are transitive verbs.

Shiroi tatemono ga mie-masu ka?	Can you see a white build-ing?
Sono oto wa kikoemasen.	I can't hear the sound.

7. The pattern denoting a negative request is formed by the plain negative form plus de *kudasai*.

Kakanaide kudasai.	Please don't write.
Tabenaide kudasai.	Please don't eat.

8. *Hō ga ii* is equivalent to English 'had better'. The dictionary form of a verb is used with this pattern. The plain past form is often used.

Yasumu hō ga ii deshō.	You had better rest.
Yasunda hō ga ii deshō.	,,
Arukanai hō ga ii to omoi-	I had better not walk, I
masu.	think.

9. The subject of a subordinate clause is followed by the postposition *ga*.

Ame ga fureba, dekake-	If it rains, I won't go out.
masen.	
Katachi ga warukereba,	If the style is bad, I don't
kaitaku nai n desu.	want to buy it.

10. *Nara* meaning 'if' can be used after the present and past form of a verb or a true adjective. This *nara* can also be used with a noun or a quasi-adjective.

Atsui nara, mado o akete	If it is hot, you may open
mo ii desu.	the window.
Anata ga iku nara, wata-	If you go, I'll go, too.
kushi mo ikimasu.	
Nihonjin nara, shitte iru	If he is a Japanese, he is
hazu desu.	expected to know it (he should know it).

LESSON XXXII

A

fútte mo even if it rains   *kakáru* take
otaku your house   *itái* painful
nisan-pun two or three minutes   *jimúsho* office
shika only (followed by negative)   *ha* tooth

B

Ame ga fureba, gakkō e kimasen ka?
Iie, ame ga futte mo, kimasu.
Kusuri o nomeba, byōki wa naorimasu ka?
Iie, aru byōki wa kusuri o nonde mo, naorimasen.

Otaku wa koko kara tōi desu ka?
Iie, tōku arimasen. Aruite mo, nisan-pun shika kakarimasen.
Samukereba, mado o shimete nete mo ii desu ka?
Iie, samukute mo, mado o akete neru hō ga ii deshō.
Ha ga itakereba, jimusho e ikimasen ka?
Iie, ha ga itakute mo, jimusho e ikimasu.

C

1. The *te*-form plus *mo* corresponds to the English expression 'even if'.

   (a) Verbs

      Dictionary form   'Even if' form

        kaku (write)   *kaite mo*
        nomu (drink)   *nonde mo*
        taberu (eat)   *tabete mo*
        suru (do)   *shite mo*
        kuru (come)   *kite mo*
        iku (go)   *itte mo*

   (b) Adjectives

        shiroi (white)   *shirokute mo*
        yasui (cheap)   *yasukute mo*

   (c) Quasi-adjectives

rippa-na (splendid)	*rippa demo*
jōzu-na (skilful)	*jōzu demo*
hontō-no (real)	*hontō demo*

Yasukute mo, kaimasen.	I won't buy it, even if it is cheap.
Jōzu demo, naratte imasu.	He is practising it, even if he is good at it.

2. The negation of the above is as follows:

kaka-nai (not to write)	*kaka-nakute mo* (even if one does not write)
tabe-nai (not to eat)	*tabe-nakute mo* („ eat)
shiroku-nai (not white)	*shiroku-nakute mo* (even if something is not white)
kirei ja (de) nai (not clean)	*kirei ja (de) nakute mo* (even if something is not clean)

3. Two numbers run together in a consecutive order:

nisan-jikan	2 or 3 hours
ichini-fun	1 or 2 minutes
goroku-nichi	5 or 6 days
shichihachi-nen	7 or 8 years
sanyo-nin	3 or 4 persons

4. The postposition *shika* is equivalent to 'only'. There is another postposition *dake*, which means 'only'. The former is used only in a negative sentence; whereas the latter can be used either in an affirmative or in a negative sentence.

Shika plus a negative is similar to *dake* plus an affirmative in meaning. There is, however, a slight difference between the two. *Shika* stresses the negative side; while *dake* the positive side.

Kanda-san dake ikimashita.	Mr. Kanda alone went.
Kanda-san dake ikimasen deshita.	Mr. Kanda was the only person who did not go.
Kanda-san shika ikimasen deshita.	Nobody went except Mr. Kanda.

When *shika* is used along with another postposition, the other postposition always stands first. When *dake* is used along with another postposition, either one may stand first.

Kanada ni shika nai n desu.	No nation has it except Canada.
Kanada ni dake aru n desu.	Canada alone has it.
Kanada dake ni aru n desu.	„

LESSON XXXIII

A

benkyō-shinákereba ikenái must study
máde ni by
kōtōgákkō senior high school
ikanákereba naránai must go
yománakute mo íi need not read
gyūnyū milk

karada health; body
ni for
hagaki post card
insatsu-suru print
kōen park
nó ni in order to
kippu ticket

B

Seito wa benkyō-shinakereba ikemasen ka?
Hai, benkyō-shinakereba ikemasen.
Anata wa nanji made ni koko e konakereba ikemasen ka?
Kuji made ni konakereba ikemasen.
Kanada no kōtōgakkō no seito wa mainichi gakkō e ikana-kereba narimasen ka?
Doyō to nichiyō no hoka wa mainichi ikanakereba narimasen.

Watakushitachi wa shinbun o yomanakereba narimasen ka?
Iie, yomanakute mo ii desu ga, yomu hō ga ii desu.
Gyūnyū o nomanakereba narimasen ka?
Hai, nomanakereba narimasen. Gyūnyū wa karada ni ii desu kara.

Hagaki ni kitte o haranakereba ikemasen ka?
Iie, haranakute mo ii desu. Kitte wa insatsu-shite arimasu.
Kōen ni hairu no ni kippu o kawanakereba narimasen ka?
Iie, kawanakute mo ii desu.

C

1. Obligation is expressed by the negative provisional form plus *ikenai* or *naranai*. The negative provisional form was dealt with before. The expression *ikenai* or *naranai* means 'it won't do'. Hence, *ikanakereba ikenai* literally means 'if one does not go, it won't do'. In other words, it means 'one must go'.

(a) Verbs

arukanai	*arukanakereba ikenai*
akenai	*akenakereba ikenai*
kinai	*kinakereba ikenai*
konai	*konakereba ikenai*
shinai	*shinakereba ikenai*

(b) Adjectives

akakunai	*akakunakereba ikenai*
atsukunai	*atsukunakereba ikenai*

(c) Quasi-adjectives

shizuka ja nai	*shizuka ja nakereba ikenai*
jōbu ja nai	*jōbu ja nakereba ikenai*

Yamanakereba ikemasen.	You have to read it.
Yoku minakereba narimasen deshita.	I had to take a good look.
Akakunakereba ikenai n desu.	It has to be red.
Jōzu ja nakereba ikemasen ka?	Do I have to be good at it?

The negative *te*-form plus *wa ikenai* (*naranai*) is sometimes used in place of the above pattern.

Ikanakute wa ikemasen.	You have to go.
Tabenakute wa ikemasen deshita ka?	Did you have to eat it?
Shirokunakute wa ikenai ka mo shiremasen.	Perhaps it may have to be white.
Kirei ja nakute wa dame deshō.	Maybe it has to be clean.

2. Care must be taken not to mix *made ni* meaning 'by' with *made* meaning 'till'.

Goji made ni kite kudasai.	Please come by 5.
Goji made hatarakimasu.	I work till 5.

3. The expression *no hoka wa* is equivalent to 'except', while *no hoka ni* as a rule means 'besides' or 'in addition to'. These two expressions are preceded by a noun.

Anata no hoka wa minna kimashita.
Everybody except you came.
Watakushi no hoka ni Suzuki-san ga ikimashita.
Mr. Suzuki besides me went.

4. The negation of obligation is expressed by the negative *te*-form plus *mo ii*.

(a) Verbs

yomanai	*yomanakute mo ii*
tabenai	*tabenakute mo ii*
minai	*minakute mo ii*
konai	*konakute mo ii*
shinai	*shinakute mo ii*

(b) Adjectives

ōkikunai	*ōkikunakute mo ii*
yasukunai	*yasukunakute mo ii*

(c) Quasi-adjectives

rippa ja nai	*rippa ja nakute mo ii*
hontō ja nai	*hontō ja nakute mo ii*

Yomanakute mo ii literally means 'even not reading is all right'. Hence, it means 'you do not have to read'.

Sonna-ni yasukunakute mo ii n desu.	It does not have to be that cheap.

Mo before *ii* is sometimes dropped.

5. The verb *hairu* demands *ni*, which is equivalent to 'in' or 'into'.

6. *No ni* is preceded by the dictionary form of a verb and corresponds to English 'in order to'. *No*, which is used for making a noun out of a verb, means 'act' or 'action'. *Kaku no ni*, therefore, means 'in the act (process) of writing'. It boils down to 'in order to write'.

Gaikokugo o hanasu no wa muzukashii desu.	To speak a foreign language is difficult.
Yomu no ni jibiki ga irimasu ka?	Do you need a dictionary in order to read it?
Soko e iku no ni chikatetsu ga ichiban benri deshō.	The subway will be most convenient for going there.

7. *No* preceded by an adjective is often equivalent to an abstract noun.

Atsui no wa kamaimasen.	I do not mind the heat.
Rippa-na no ni odoroku deshō.	You will be surprised at the splendor.

LESSON XXXIV

A

oyá parents	*kyakuma* drawing room
ni by	*saifu* purse; wallet
shikararemásu (*shikarareru*) be scolded	*tóru* pick; rob
itazura mischief	*nándomo* many times
útsu shoot	*machigái* error; mistake
homéru praise	*naósu* correct; fix
shōsetsuka novelist	*hazukashíi* be ashamed; bashful
shiru know	*tama-ni* once in a while
okyaku guest	*kása* umbrella
daidokoro kitchen	*nurete shimaimásu* get wet completely
tō(óo)su usher; show	

B

Kodomo wa tokidoki oya ni shikararemasu ka?
Hai, shikararemasu. Itazura o shimasu kara.
Rinkān wa dare ni utaremashita ka?
Būsu to iu hito ni utaremashita.
Donna seito ga sensei ni homeraremasu ka?
Yoku benkyō-suru seito ga homeraremasu.
Shōsetsuka no Mōmu wa Kanadajin ni shirarete imasu ka?
Hai, shirarete iru to omoimasu.
Okyaku wa taitei daidokoro e tōsaremasu ka?
Iie, daidokoro e tōsaremasen. Kyakuma e tōsaremasu.

Anata wa saifu o torareta koto ga arimasu ka?
Iie, mada torareta koto ga arimasen.
Anata wa sensei ni nandomo machigai o naosaremasu ka?
Hai, nandomo naosarete, hazukashii desu.
Tomodachi ni korarete, benkyō dekinai koto ga arimasu ka?
Hai, tama-ni arimasu.
Ame ni furarete, kasa ga nakereba, dō narimasu ka?
Tabun nurete shimaimasu.

C

1. The Japanese passive voice differs greatly from the English in that the subject of the passive verb is, in most cases, a human being or a living creature.

2. The passive voice is formed in the following way:

(a) Group I Verbs (1st base plus *reru*)

Dictionary form	Passive
kiku (ask)	*kikareru*
yobu (call)	*yobareru*
shikaru (scold)	*shikarareru*
warau (laugh)	*warawareru*

(b) Group II Verbs (1st base plus *rareru*)

| *homeru* (praise) | *homerareru* |
| *miru* (see) | *mirareru* |

(c) Irregular Verbs

| *kuru* (come) | *korareru* |
| *suru* (do) | *sareru* |

3. The person who is affected by the action is denoted by the postposition *wa* or *ga*. The agent or the person by whom an action is performed in the passive voice is denoted by the postposition *ni*. The thing on which the action is performed is denoted by a noun plus the postposition *o*.

Watakushi wa yobaremashita.	I was called.
Kodomo wa okāsan ni shika- *rareru deshō.*	The child will be scolded by his mother.
Ano kata wa dorobō ni kaban *o toraremashita.*	He had his suitcase stolen by a thief.

4. The first two sentences in 3. can be called the direct passive. The last sentence can be called the indirect passive, in which the animate subject is followed by *wa* or *ga* and the object of the verb by *o*.

'*Ano kata no kaban wa dorobō ni toraremashita.*' is the word-for-word translation of 'His suitcase was stolen by a thief.' and is far from idiomatic. Idiomatic Japanese demands that the subject should be *ano kata*, resulting in a slight change in the construction.

5. What strikes the English-speaking people as strange is that Japanese intransitive verbs such as *kuru* (come), *furu* (rain or snow), *yameru* (quit), *shinu* (die), etc., can form the passive voice with the unfavorable shade of meaning. In other words, a passive formed by intransitive verbs denotes 'be unfavorably affected by someone else's action'.

| *Hisho ni yameraremashita.* | My secretary quit on me. |
| *Ojōsan ni shinaremashita.* | He lost his daughter. |

(Lit. He was unfavorably affected by his daughter's dying.)

Ano hito wa watakushi no   He picked my purse (wallet).
saifu o torimashita.
Watakushi no saifu wa ano   My purse was picked by
hito ni toraremashita.   him.

If the word *watakushi* is to be used as the subject of the above sentence, there takes place a little change in the construction.

Watakushi wa ano hito ni   I had my purse picked by
saifu o toraremashita.   him.

6.   The Japanese passive is often used in a potential sense. This is particularly the case with Group II verbs. Generally speaking, a potential sense is indicated when an inanimate object is the subject of a sentence. It should be remembered that the context holds the key to determining whether the form is passive or potential.

Kore wa taberaremasen.   This is not edible.
Sono fuku wa chiisakute   That suit is small and
kirarenai n desu.   can't be worn.
Ikarenai to iimashita ka?   Did he say that he could
   not go?

The passive construction is sometimes employed in expressing a polite sense.

Takushī ni noraremashita ka?   Did you take a cab?
Kaigi ni deraremasu ka?   Would you attend the conference?

7.   The postposition *no* is used when two nouns are in apposition.

shōsetsuka no Mōmu   Maugham, the novelist
shichō no Ikeda-san   Mr. Ikeda, the mayor
daitōryō no Kenedi-san   Mr. Kennedy, the president

8.   The pattern *koto ga aru* preceded by the plain past form of a verb denotes the past experience. *Koto ga aru* literally means 'there is a fact or occasion'.

Tabeta koto ga arimasu.   I have eaten it.

Kiita koto ga arimasen.   I have never heard it.

Nihon e itta koto ga arimasu ka?   Have you ever been to Japan?

9. When preceded by the dictionary form of a verb or an adjective, the pattern *koto ga aru* means 'sometimes'. Very often the postposition *ga* is replaced by *mo*.

Kuji goro yūhan o taberu koto ga arimasu.   I sometimes eat supper about 9.

Jūgatsu ni samui koto ga arimasu.   It is sometimes cold in October.

10. The terminal verb *shimau* used after the *te*-form adds a tone of completeness or finality to the meaning of the *te*-form. *Shimau* as a regular verb means 'finish up'.

Wasurete shimaimashita.   I have completely forgotten it.

LESSON XXXV

A

jibun de by oneself

migaku polish; brush

ítsumo always

otōto younger brother

migakaseru make one polish

oishasan medical doctor

byōnin sick person

shōgákkō elementary school

mátsu wait

késshite never (followed by negative)

okóru get angry

okā(áa)san mother

kudámono fruit

yasai vegetable

tamágo egg

kánai ones' own wife

kai ni iku go to buy

B

Anata wa jibun de kutsu o migakimasu ka?

Iie, itsumo otōto ni migakasemasu.

Oishasan wa byōnin ni bīru o nomasemasu ka?

Iie, nomasenai deshō.

Kanada no shōgakkō de wa, sensei wa seito ni hon o yomasemasu ka?

Sensei wa warui seito o tatasemasu ka?

Anata wa tomodachi o matasemasu ka?
Onna no tomodachi nara, kesshite matasemasen. Mataseru
to, okorimasu kara.
Okāsan wa akachan ni niku o tabesasemasu ka?
Tabesasenai deshō.
Donata ni kudamono ya yasai ya tamago o kawasemasu ka?
Kanai ni kawasemasu ga, jibun de kai ni iku koto mo ari-
masu.

C

1. The basic idea of the causative is that a person causes some
other person or living creature to do something. Japanese
causative verbs do not imply that someone has an action performed for him as a favor.

Chōnan ni tegami o kakase- *mashita.*	I made my eldest son write the letter.

Compare the above sentence with the following:

Ano kata ni tegami o kaite *moraimashita.*	I had him write the letter. — he did it as a favor.
Ano kata ni tegami o kaka- *semashita.*	I had him write the letter. — I ordered him to do it.

In other words, the idea of a favor must be expressed not
by a causative form, but by an entirely different form.

2. The causative form is made in the following way:
(a) Group I Verbs (1st base plus *seru*)

Dictionary form	Causative
kaku (write)	*kakaseru*
yomu (read)	*yomaseru*

matsu (wait)	*mataseru*
kau (buy)	*kawaseru*

(b) Group II Verbs (1st base plus *saseru*)

taberu (eat)	*tabesaseru*
kiru (wear)	*kisaseru*

(c) Irregular Verbs

kuru (come)	*kosaseru*
suru (do)	*saseru*

The causative is sometimes expressed by the shorter form *su* instead of *seru*: *kakasu* for *kakaseru*, *tabesasu* for *tabesaseru*, *sasu* for *saseru*, etc.

3. The person who causes the action is denoted by the postposition *wa* or *ga*. The agent or the person who is caused to perform the action is denoted by the postposition *ni*. The noun denoting the direct object of the action itself is followed by the postposition *o*.

Watakushi wa matasemashita.	I made him wait.
Anata ni kakasemasu ka?	Does he make you write it?
Hanamachi-san wa watakushi ni hon o yomasemasen.	Mr. Hanamachi won't let me read the book.

4. If the causative is based on an intransitive verb, the person who is made to perform the action is, in most cases, denoted by the postposition *o*.

Kodomo o arukasenaide kudasai.	Please don't make the child walk.
Okyaku o matasete wa ikemasen.	You must not make your guest wait. (Don't keep your guest waiting.)

5. The postposition *wa* of *de wa* indicates the topic of the sentence.

Tōkyō de wa nanji goro kuraku narimasu ka?	About what time does it become dark in Tokyo?

Bankūbā ni wa ii mise ga taku-san arimasu.	In Vancouver there are many good stores.

6. The word *kesshite* is used with a negative word.

Kesshite matasemasen.	They never keep you waiting.

7. *Ni* indicates the purpose, when followed by such verbs of motion as *iku* (go), *kuru* (come), *dekakeru* (go out), *deru* (leave), *kaeru* (return), etc. This *ni* is preceded by the 2nd base of verbs.

Kashiya o sagashi ni ikima-shita.	He went to hunt for a house for rent.
Ohirugohan o tabe ni dekaketa kamo shiremasen.	He may have gone out to eat lunch.
Asobi ni kite kudasai.	Come and see me, please.

This construction is used with a noun too:

Kaimono ni dekakemashita.	She went out to do shopping.
Sanpo ni ikimasen ka?	Won't you go for a walk?

LESSON XXXVI

A

misé store	*resutoran* restaurant
matasaréru be kept waiting	*katái* tough; hard
kónde iru (*komu*) be crowded	*tabitabi* often
ed	*otō* (*óo*) *san* father
kirai désu dislike	*sōji-suru* clean; sweep

B

Anata wa mise de matasaremasu ka?
Hai, mise ga konde ireba, matasaremasu.

Matasareru no wa suki desu ka, kirai desu ka?
Matasareru no wa kirai desu.
Kanada de wa, seito wa sensei ni hon o yomasaremasu ka?
Hai, seito wa sensei ni hon o yomasaremasu.

Resutoran de katai niku o tabesaserareta koto ga arimasu ka?
Hai, tabesaserareta koto ga arimasu.
Kodomo wa tabitabi otōsan ni heya o sōjisaseraremasu ka?
Hai, sōjisaseraremasu.

C

1. The passive causative means the passive made from a
causative. This construction denotes literally 'be made to do'.

(a) Group I Verbs

Causative	Passive causative
nomaseru (make one drink)	*nomaserareru*
nomasu	*nomasareru*
kikaseru (make one hear)	*kikaserareru*
kikasu	*kikasareru*

(b) Group II Verbs

tabesaseru (make one eat)	*tabesaserareru*
tabesasu	*tabesasareru*

(c) Irregular Verbs

kosaseru (make one come)	*kosaserareru*
kosasu	*kosasareru*
saseru (make one do)	*saserareru*
sasu	*sasareru*

2. The formation of the passive form was discussed before. As
the above indicates, there are two forms of the passive causative verbs. In the case of Group I verbs, the shorter form is

more frequently used; however, in the case of Group II verbs and Irregular verbs, the longer form occurs more frequently.

Matasaremashita ka?	Were you made to wait?
Furui pan o tabesaseraremasu.	You are made to eat stale bread.
Watakushi wa sensei ni saku-bun o kakasaremashita.	I was made to write a composition by my teacher.

LESSON XXXVII

A

imōto younger sister
kowáretara (kowareru) when (if) it breaks
tokeiya watch - m a k e r's; watch-maker
mótte iku take
tokoya barber shop; barber
hige moustache; beard
sóru shave
kamí hair
karú trim; clip
dake only
shinju pearl

yubiwa ring
komátte iru (komaru) be in trouble
tasukéru help
dekiru dake as much as possible
monó thing
koshiraeru make
hotóndo almost
appuru-pai apple-pie
métta-ni seldom (followed by negative)

B

Anatawa itsumo jibun de tegami o dashimasu ka?
Iie, itsumo imōto ni dashite moraimasu.
Tokei ga kowaretara, dō shimasu ka?
Tokeiya e motte itte, naoshite moraimasu.
Tokoya de hige o sotte moraimasu ka?
Iie, sotte moraimasen. Kami dake katte moraimasu.

Okāsan no tanjōbi ni nani o katte agetai desu ka?

Shinju no yubiwa o katte agetai to omoimasu.
Tomodachi ga komatte iru toki ni, tasukete agemasu ka?
Hai, dekiru dake tasukete agemasu.
Okāsan wa mainichi oishii mono o koshiraete kudasaimasu
ka?
Hai, hotondo mainichi koshiraete kudasaimasu.
Anata wa mise de appuru-pai o kaimasu ka?
Iie, kanai ga tsukutte kuremasu kara, metta-ni kaimasen.

C

1. In the following diagrams **S** indicates the subject of a sentence
and the arrow points away from the giver:

(a) Diagram 1   *ageru*; *yaru*; *sashiageru* (give)

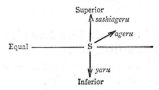

Giver *wa* + Receiver [equal or superior] *ni* + *ageru*
       ga
Giver *wa* + Receiver [inferior] *ni* + *yaru*
       ga
Giver *wa* + Receiver [superior or equal] *ni* + *sashiageru*
       ga
The following situations are possible (1 — 1st person; 2 — 2nd
person; 3 — 3rd person):
 1 → 2   1 → 3   2 → 3   3 → 3
Examples:
(1 → 2) *Watakushi wa anata ni kore o agemashita.*
         I gave this to you.
(1 → 3) *Watakushi wa kodomo ni omocha o yarimashita.*
         I gave the child a toy.
(2 → 3) *Anata wa Tada-san ni kore o sashiagemasu ka?*
         Will you give this to Mr. Tada?
(3 → 3) *Toyota-san ga Honda-san ni enpitsu o ageta n desu.*
         Mr. Toyota gave Mr. Honda a pencil.

(b) Diagram 2 *morau*; *itadaku* (receive)

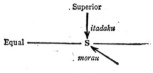

Receiver *wa* + Giver [equal or inferior] *kara* (or *ni*) + *morau*
        ga
Receiver *wa* + Giver [superior or equal] *kara* (or *ni*) + *itadaku*
        ga

The following situations are possible:

1 ← 2   2 ← 1   3 ← 1
1 ← 3   2 ← 3   3 ← 2
                      3 ← 3

Examples:

(1 ← 2) *Watakushi wa anata kara kore o moraimashita.*
         I got this from you.
(1 ← 3) *Watakushi wa ano kata kara tokei o itadakimashita.*
         I got a watch from him.
(2 ← 1) *Anata wa watakushi ni sore o moratta n desu.*
         You got it from me.
(2 ← 3) *Anata wa Yada-san kara okurimono o itadaku deshō.*
         Perhaps you will get a gift from Mr. Yada.
(3 ← 1) *Kono ko wa watakushi kara kore o morawanakatta n desu.*
         This child did not get this from me.
(3 ← 2) *Honda-san wa anata ni kore o moratta n desu.*
         Mr. Honda got this from you.
(3 ← 3) *Ano hito wa tomodachi kara tegami o moratta n desu ka?*
         Did he get a letter from a friend of his?

(c) Diagram 3 *kureru*; *kudasaru* (give)

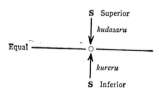

Giver [equal or inferior] *wa* + Receiver *ni* + *kureru*
             ga
Giver [superior or equal] *wa* + Receiver *ni* + *kudasaru*
             ga

Note that the giver is some one else, not the speaker and that the receiver is the speaker or somebody in his group (e.g. family member, relative, colleague, friend, acquaintance, compatriot, etc.)
The following situations are possible:

2→1   2→3   3→3
3→1   3→2

Examples:

(2→1)   *Anata ga watakushi ni kore o kudasaimashita.*
          You gave this to me.
(3→1)   *Honda-san wa watakushi ni kami o kureru deshō.*
          Perhaps Mr. Honda will give me a sheet of paper.
(2→3)   *Anata ga watakushi no kodomo ni chokorēto o kureta n desu ka?*
          Did you give my child a bar of chocolate?
(3→2)   *Ano hito wa anata ni kippu o kureru deshō.*
          He will perhaps give you a ticket.
(3→3)   *Aru gaijin ga Nihonjin ni kore o kureta n desu.*
          A certain foreigner gave this to a Japanese.

2. When the verbs *ageru*; *yaru*; *sashiageru*; *morau*; *itadaku*; *kureru*; *kudasaru* are used after the *te*-form, the original meaning of these verbs is lost, but the function of specifying who does something and for whom something is done is retained.

(a) The terminal verb *ageru* preceded by the *te*-form means that a person does a favor for an equal or a superior in social status, age, etc.

The terminal verb *yaru* preceded by the *te*-form means that a person does a favor for an inferior in social status, age, etc.

The terminal verb *sashiageru* preceded by the *te*-form means that a person does a favor for a superior or an equal in social status, age, etc.

The above boils down to:

Giver *wa* + Receiver [equal or superior] *ni* + *...te ageru*
        ga

Giver *wa* + Receiver [inferior] *ni* + ...*te yaru*
    ga

Giver *wa* + Receiver [superior or equal] *ni* + ...*te sashiageru*
    ga

Examples:

(1 → 2)   *Watakushi ga anata ni sore o kaite agemasu.*
       I'll write it for you.

(1 → 3)   *Watakushi wa sono ko ni ningyō o katte yarimashita.*
       I bought a doll for the child.

(2 → 3)   *Anata wa ojisan ni kore o misete sashiagemashita ka?* .
       Did you show this to your uncle?

(3 → 3)   *Otōsan wa musuko ni eigo o oshiete yarimasuka?*
       Does the father teach his son English?

(b)   The terminal verb *morau* preceded by the *te*-form means that a person has a favor done for him by an equal or an inferior in social status, age, etc.

The terminal verb *itadaku* preceded by the *te*-form means that a person has a favor done for him by a superior or an equal in social status, age, etc.

The above boils down to:

Receiver *wa* + Giver [equal or inferior] *ni* + ...*te morau*
    ga

Receiver *wa* + Giver [superior or equal] *ni* + ...*te itadaku*
    ga

Examples:

(1 ← 2)   *Watakushi wa anata ni kutsu o migaite moraimashita.*
       I had you shine my shoes.

(1 ← 3)   *Watakushi wa Hondo-san ni michi o oshiete itadakimasu.*
       I'll have Mr. Honda show me the way.

(2 ← 1)   *Anata wa watakushi ni soko e itte moraitai n desu ka?*
       Do you want me to go there?

(2 ← 3)   *Anata wa otōsan ni kono kuruma o katte itadaita n desu ka?*
       Did you have your father buy this car?

(3 ← 1)   *Ano hito wa watakushi ni kore o aratte moraitai n deshō.*
       Perhaps he wants me to wash this.

(3 ← 2) *Yada-san wa anata ni kore o naoshitemoratta n desu.*
        Mr. Yada had you fix this.

(3 ← 3) *Otōto wa choichoi niisan ni omoi mono o motte moraimasu.*
        The younger brother often has his brother carry heavy
        things.

(c) The terminal verb *kureru* preceded by the *te*-form means that
an equal or an inferior in social status, age, etc. does a favor for
the speaker or somebody in his group (e.g., family member, relative,
colleague, friend, acquaintance, compatriot, etc.).

The terminal verb *kudasaru* preceded by the *te*-form means that
a superior or an equal in social status, age, etc. does a favor for
the speaker or somebody in his group (e.g. family member, relative,
colleague, friend, acquaintance, compatriot, etc.).

The above boils down to:

Giver [equal or inferior] *wa* + Receiver *ni* + ...*te kureru*
                            ga

Giver [superior or equal] *wa* + Receiver *ni* + ...*te kudasaru*
                            ga

Examples:

(2 → 1) *Anata wa watakushi ni chizu o kaite kuremasu ka?*
        Will you be kind enough to draw the map for me?

(3 → 1) *Ano kata no okāsan wa watakushi ni kono hana o okutte
        kudasaimashita.*
        Her mother was kind enough to send me these
        flowers.

(2 → 3) *Anata ga kodomo ni kore o tsukutte kureta n desu ka?*
        Did you make this for my child?

(3 → 2) *Honda-san ga anata ni nihongo o oshiete kureru deshō.*
        Perhaps Mr. Honda will be good enough to teach you
        Japanese.

(3 → 3) *Aru gaijin wa watakushi no tomodachi ni yūhan o gochisō-
        shite kuremashita.*
        A certain foreigner was kind enough to treat a friend
        of mine to supper.

3. Note that in talking to some one else who is not a member of his
family a person should not use any words indicating deference when

referring to a member of his family who is superior and older.
In the following dialogue A is not a member of B's family, therefore B uses *moratta* (not *itadaita*) in a.; *kureta* (not *kudasatta*) in b.;
agemasu (not *sashiagemasu*) in c., even though he refers to his father
who is superior and older.

a. A: *Otōsan ni itadaita n desu ka?*
          Did you get it from your father?
     B: *Ee, chichi ni moratta n desu.*
          Yes, I got it from him.

b. A: *Otōsan ga kudasatta n desu ka?*
          Did your father give it to you?
     B: *Ee, chichi ga kureta n desu.*
          Yes, he gave it to me.

c. A: *Otōsan ni sashiagemasu ka?*
          Will you give it to your father?
     B: *Ee, chichi ni agemasu.*
          Yes, I will give it to him.

4. The conditional meaning (1) 'if so-and-so should happen'
or 'if so-and-so should be the case' and (2) 'when so-and-so
happens' is formed by the plain past of verbs, adjectives, and
copula plus *ra*.

Verbs:

(a) Group I

Plain past	Conditional
kaita (wrote)	*kaitara* (if he should write or when he writes)
nonda (drank)	*nondara*
futta (rained; snowed)	*futtara*
itta (went)	*ittara*

(b) Group II

tabeta (ate)	*tabetara*
mita (saw)	*mitara*

(c) Irregular

kita came)	*kitara*
shita (did)	*shitara*

Adjectives:

samukatta	*samukattara* (if it should be cold or when it is
ōkikatta	cold)
nakatta	*ōkikattara*
	nakattara

Copula:

datta	*dattara* (if . . . should be or when . . . is)

Ame ga futtara, konai deshō.	If it should rain, he would not come.
Kitara, issho-ni ikimashō.	If he should come, (when he comes,) let's go together.
Ii tenki dattara, ikitai n desu.	If it should be fine weather, I would like to go.
Watakushi dattara, sonna koto o shimasen ga.	If I were you, I would not do such a thing.
Shigoto ga owattara, denwa-shimasu.	When the work is completed, I'll give you a ring.

The conditional refers to the present, the future, or the past. The predicate of the final clause, a time word, or the general situation—in final analysis, the context will determine the exact meaning.

5. The subjunctive which is a condition or supposition contrary to fact is often expressed by the use of *tara*.

Mō sukoshi yasukattara, kau n desu ga.	If it were a little cheaper, I would buy it.
Okane ga attara, kau n desu ga.	If I had money, I would buy it.

Okane ga attara, katta n desu ga.   If I had had money, I would have bought it.

6. The subjunctive can also be expressed as follows:

Kuruma ga areba, iku no ni.   If I had a car, I would go.
Kuruma ga areba, itta no ni.   If I had had a car, I would have gone.

7. The expression *metta-ni* is used with a negative word.

Metta-ni kimasen.   He seldom comes.

8. Supplementary notes on *to; toki (ni); eba; tara*

To (whenever; if; when)

(1) This *to* must be preceded by a present-tense form, even when the final clause is in the past tense. The *to* clause usually refers to a general condition, because the final predicate denotes repeated or habitual action.

Haru ga kuru to, sakimasu.   It is in bloom whenever spring comes.

Samui to, yuki ga furimasu.   Whenever (if) it is cold, it snows.

(2) If the final clause is in the past tense, the *to* clause is translated as 'when'.

Gakkō ga owaru to, uchi ni kaerimashita.   When school was over, I went home.

(3) This *to* cannot be used, if the final clause denotes command (*nasai*); request (*te kudasai*); invitation (*mashō; mashō ka*); advice (*hō ga ii*); intention (*tsumori desu*), etc.

(4) Either *eba* or *tara* should be used for (3).

Toki (ni) (when; while)

The *toki* clause usually refers to a particular point or period of time. Either the present or the past may be used before the word *toki*.

Kōhī o nomitai toki ni, kono mise ni kimasu.   When I want to have a cup of coffee, I come to this shop.

Tōkyō ni ita toki ni,	I bought it when (while) I was
katta n desu.	in Tokyo.

Eba (if; when)

(1) Whenever the reference is to a present state of affairs, or to a definite happening in the future, *eba* is translated as 'if'.

Anata ga ikeba,	If you go, I'll go too.
watashi mo ikimasu.	
Samukereba, mado o	If you are cold, please shut the
shimete kudasai.	windows

(2) Whenever the reference is to a happening in the past, or when it occurs in a general statement referring to either repeated acts or a continued condition, *eba* is translated as 'when'.

Ame ga fureba,	When it rained,
uchi ni imashita.	I stayed at home.
Sakura ga sakeba,	When the cherryblossoms come out,
minna mi ni ikimasu.	everybody goes to view them.

(3) In many situations *eba* and *tara* are interchangeable.

Yokereba, kaitai n desu.	If it is good, I would like to buy it.
Yokattara, kaitai n desu.	If it should be good, I would like to buy it.

The *tara* clause often suggests some doubt whether so-and-so will happen or not, whereas the *eba* clause suggests nothing about the likelihood of the event, but merely says that if one thing happens, then another thing will happen too.

Tara (if; when)

(1) If the final clause is non-definite (i.e., indicating doubt or referring to the future), the *tara* clause shows pure supposition. This supposition may refer to the present, future or past. This *tara* is translated as 'if'. In this case *tara* and *eba* are interchangeable.

Ame ga yandara, ikimasu.	If it should stop raining, I would go.
Basu ga tomarebo, orimasu.	If the bus stops, I'll get off.

(2) If the final clause is definite (i.e., referring to a past or present completion), the *tara* clause is a statement of actual fact. This *tara* is translated as 'when'.

Kusuri o nondara, When I took medicine, I got well.
naorimashita,

Basu gatomattara, Let's get off when the bus (has)
orimashō. stopped.

The *tara* clause envisages 'completion', but the *eba* clause does not.

(3) The word *moshi*, which is sometimes employed in the *tara* or *eba* clause, serves as a sort of warning that the speaker is going to use the conditional or provisional form.

Moshi takakattara, If it should be expensive,
kawanaide kudasai. please do not buy it.

LESSON XXXVIII

A

akeru yō(óo) ni iu *kóe* voice
 tell one to open *suu* smoke; inhale
jū(úu)sho address *osshaimásu (ossharu)* say

B

"Mado o akete kudasai." to iimashita.
Mado o akeru yō ni iimashita.

"Namae to jūsho o kaite kudasai." to iimasu.
Namae to jūsho o kaku yō ni iimasu.

"Ōkii koe de hanasanaide kudasai." to itte kudasai.
Ōkii koe de hanasanai yō ni itte kudasai.

Oishasan wa tabako o suu yō ni osshaimasu ka, suwanai yō ni osshaimasu ka?
Tabun suwanai yō ni ossharu deshō.

Nanji ni kuru yō ni iimashō ka?
Goji ni kuru yō ni itte kudasai.

C

1. In quoting what is said or written either (a) the exact words that were used or (b) the gist of the speech or thought can be given.

(a) *"Yuki ga futte imasu." to iimashita.*
He said, "It's snowing."

(b) *Yuki ga futte iru to iimashita.*
He said that it was snowing.

(c) *"Ame ga futte imasu ka?" to iimashita.*
"Is it raining?" he said.

(d) *Ame ga futte iru ka (to) kikimashita.*
He asked me if it was raining.

The final predicate of the quoted sentence is generally in the plain form.

2. It is sometimes difficult to distinguish the direct quotation from the indirect quotation in Japanese, which is also the case with English (e.g. 'I said forget about it.').

No sequence of tenses occurs in Japanese, as is shown in the above examples.

3. A quotation containing 'please do so-and-so' can be expressed by the use of *yō ni* preceded by the dictionary form of a verb in indirect narration. The expression *yō ni* literally means 'in such a manner or way'.

(a) *"Mō sukoshi yukkuri hanashite kudasai." to iimashita.*
She said, "Please speak a little more slowly."

(b) *Mō sukoshi yukkuri hanasu yō ni iimashita.*
She told me to speak a little more slowly.

(c) *"Machi nasai." to iimashita.*
He said, "Wait."

(d) *Matsu yō ni iimashita.*
He told me to wait.

(e) *"Tabenaide kudasai." to iimashita.*
He said, "Please don't eat it."

(f) *Tabenai yō ni iimashita.*
He told me not to eat it.

4. The verb *ossharu* is the honorific form of the verb *iu.* Honorific words are used in speaking of a superior, and humble words are used in speaking of oneself or of an inferior. The humble form of the verb *iku* is *ukagau.* The honorific form of *iku* is *irassharu.*

5. Note the following Group I honorific verbs:

Dictionary form	2nd base
gozaru (be; have)	*gozaimasu*
irassharu (be; go; come)	*irasshaimasu*
kudasaru (give)	*kudasaimasu*
nasaru (do)	*nasaimasu*
ossharu (say)	*osshaimasu*

ENGLISH TRANSLATION OF SECTION B SENTENCES

LESSON I

Kore wa hon desu.
Sore wa kami desu ka?
Hai, sore wa kami desu.
Kore wa isu desu ka?
Iie, kore wa isu ja arimasen.
Are wa isu ja arimasen.
Kore wa nan desu ka?
Sore wa zasshi desu.
Are wa tsukue desu ka, isu desu ka?
Are wa tsukue desu.
Kore mo hon desu.
Sore mo kami desu ka?
Are mo tsukue ja arimasen.

This is a book.
Is that a sheet of paper?
Yes, it (that) is a sheet of paper.
Is this a chair?
No, this is not a chair.
That over there is not a chair.
What is this?
It (that) is a magazine.
Is that over there a desk or a chair?
It (that over there) is a desk.
This also is a book.
Is that also a sheet of paper?
That over there is not a desk either.

LESSON II

Watakushi wa Yamakawa desu.
Anata wa Jōnzu-san desu ka?
Iie, sō ja arimasen.
Ano kata wa Kanadajin desu ka?
Hai, sō desu.
Ikeda-san wa Nihonjin desu ka, Amerikajin desu ka?
Ikeda-san wa Nihonjin desu.
Anata wa gakusei desu.
Jōnzu-san mo gakusei desu ka?
Horando-san wa gakusei desu ka, sensei desu ka?
Horando-san wa gakusei ja arimasen. Sensei desu.
Anata wa donata desu ka?

I am Yamakawa.
Are you Mr. Jones?
No, I am not.
Is he a Canadian?
Yes, he is.
Is Mr. Ikeda a Japanese or an American?
He (Mr. Ikeda) is a Japanese.
You are a student.
Is Mr. Jones a student too?
Is Mr. Holland a student or a teacher?
He (Mr. Holland) is not a student. He is a teacher.
Who are you?

91

LESSON III

Kore wa akai hon desu.
Sore wa shiroi kami desu ka?
Are wa ōkii hako ja arimasen.
Kore mo nagai enpitsu desu ka?
Sore mo mijikai enpitsu desu.
Are mo chiisai hako ja arimasen.

Kore wa akai enpitsu desu ka, kiiroi enpitsu desu ka?
Sore wa akai enpitsu desu. Kiiroi enpitsu ja arimasen.

This is a red book.
Is that a sheet of white paper?
That over there is not a big box.
Is this also a long pencil?
That also is a short pencil.
That over there is not a small box either.
Is this a red pencil or a yellow pencil?
It (that) is a red pencil. It is not a yellow pencil.

LESSON IV

Honoruru wa samui desu ka?
Iie, samuku arimasen. Atsui desu.
Arasuka wa atsui desu ka?
Iie, atsuku arimasen.
Kono hon wa akai desu ka?
Iie, akaku arimasen. Aoi desu.
Sono hako wa ōkii desu ka?
Iie, ōkiku arimasen. Chiisai desu.
Ano kaban wa kuroi desu ka, shiroi desu ka?
Kuroi desu.
Sono ōkii hon wa takai desu ka, yasui desu ka?
Takai desu.
Kono hankachi wa shiroi desu ka?
Kono enpitsu wa nagaku arimasen ka?
Hai, nagaku arimasen.

Is Honolulu cold?
No, it is not. It is hot.
Is Alaska hot?
No, it is not.
Is this book red?
No, it is not. It is blue.
Is that box big?
No, it is not. It is small.
Is that suitcase over there black or white?
It is black.
Is that big book expensive or cheap?
It is expensive.
Is this handkerchief white?
Isn't this pencil long?

No, it is not.

LESSON V

Watakushi no kutsu wa kuroi desu.
Anata no uwagi wa aoi desu ka?
Iie, aoku arimasen.
Jōnzu-san no zubon wa donna iro desu ka?
Jōnzu-san no zubon wa kuroi desu.

My shoes are black.
Is your coat blue?
No, it is not.
What color are Mr. Jones' pants?

They are black.

Ano kata no mannenhitsu wa akaku arimasen ka?	Isn't his fountain-pen red?
Hai, akaku arimasen. Kuroi desu.	No, it is not. It is black.
Ano kata no bōshi wa donna iro desu ka?	What color is his hat?
Anata no kutsu wa kuroi desu ne.	Your shoes are black, aren't they?
Watakushi no kutsu mo kuroi desu.	My shoes are black too.
Ano kata no kutsu mo shiroku arimasen.	His shoes are not white either.

LESSON VI

Kore wa anata no desu ka?	Is this yours?
Hai, watakushi no desu.	Yes, it is mine.
Sono hon wa watakushi no desu ka?	Is that book mine?
Iie, anata no ja arimasen.	No, it is not.
Kono jibiki wa donata no desu ka?	Whose is this dictionary?
Ishiyama-san no desu.	It is Mr. Ishiyama's.
Ano tokei wa kono kata no desu ka?	Does that watch over there belong to this person?
Iie, kono kata no ja arimasen. Ano kata no desu.	No, it does not. It belongs to that person over there.

LESSON VII

enpitsu to kami	a pencil and a sheet of paper
sensei to seito	a teacher and a pupil
ōkii tsukue to chiisai isu	a big desk and a small chair
Kanadajin to Amerikajin to Nihonjin	Canadians, Americans and Japanese
Kono enpitsu to kami wa donata no desu ka?	Whose are these pencils and sheets of paper?
Watakushi no desu.	They are mine.
Sensei to seito wa Kanadajin desu ka?	Are the teacher and pupils Canadians?
Iie, sensei wa Nihonjin de, seito wa Kanadajin desu.	No, the teacher is a Japanese and the pupils are Canadians.
Kore wa watakushi no hon de, sore wa anata no hon desu.	This is my book and that is your book.

LESSON VIII

Buritisshu Koronbia Daigaku wa doko ni arimasu ka?	Where is the University of British Columbia?
Bankūbā ni arimasu.	It is in Vancouver.
Keiō Daigaku wa Bankūbā ni arimasen.	Keiō University is not in Vancouver.
Anata no enpitsu wa koko ni arimasu ka?	Is your pencil here?
Iie, koko ni arimasen.	No, it is not.
Watakushi no jibiki wa soko ni arimasu ka?	Is my dictionary there?
Iie, arimasen.	No, it is not.
Ikeda-san no uchi wa asuko ni arimasu ka?	Is Mr. Ikeda's house over there?
Watakushi no hankachi wa poketto no naka ni arimasu.	My handkerchief is in my pocket.
Akai hon wa doko ni arimasu ka?	Where is the red book?
Tsukue no ue ni arimasu.	It is on the desk.
Howaito-san no kaban wa isu no ue ni arimasu ka?	Is Mr. White's suitcase on the chair?
Iie, isu no shita ni arimasu.	No, it is under the chair.
Anata no uchi wa gakkō no soba ni arimasu ka?	Is your house by the school?
Hai, sō desu. Chikai desu.	Yes, it is. It is near.
Ano kata no zasshi wa tsukue no ue ni arimasu ka, shita ni arimasu ka?	Is his magazine on the desk, or under it?
Tsukue no ue ni arimasu.	It is on the desk.
Tsukue wa doko ni arimasu ka?	Where is the desk?
Tsukue wa anata no mae ni arimasu.	It is in front of you.
Kokuban wa watakushi no mae ni arimasu ka?	Is the blackboard in front of me?
Iie, anata no ushiro ni arimasu.	No, it is behind you.

LESSON IX

Tsukue no ue ni shinbun ga arimasu.	There is a newspaper on the desk.
Kaban no naka ni nani ga arimasu ka?	What is in the suitcase?
Hon to kami to enpitsu ga arimasu.	There are a book, paper and a pencil in it.

Isu no shita ni anata no zasshi ga arimasu ka? Is your magazine under the chair?

Iie, arimasen. No, it is not.

Kono hako no naka ni nani ga arimasu ka? What is in this box?

Nannimo arimasen. There is nothing in it.

Kono heya ni mado ga ikutsu arimasu ka? How many windows are there in this room?

Yottsu arimasu. There are four.

Doa mo yottsu arimasu ka? Are there four doors too?

Iie, doa wa yottsu arimasen. Futatsu arimasu. No, there are not four doors. There are two.

Bankūbā ni depāto ga ikutsu arimasu ka? How many department stores are there in Vancouver?

Bankūbā ni depāto ga mittsu arimasu. There are three department stores in Vancouver.

LESSON X

Kabin no naka ni kirei-na hana ga arimasu. There are beautiful flowers in the vase.

Kono hana wa kirei desu nē. These flowers are beautiful, aren't they?

Akai hana wa ikutsu arimasu ka? How many red flowers are there?

Muttsu arimasu. There are six.

Shiroi hana mo muttsu arimasu ka? Are there six white flowers too?

Iie, muttsu arimasen. Yattsu arimasu. No, there are not. There are eight.

Watakushi wa Nihonjin desu ga, anatagata wa Kanadajin desu. I am Japanese, but (and) you are Canadians.

Tsukue wa hitotsu arimasu ga, isu wa takusan arimasu. There is one desk, but there are many chairs.

Tōkyō wa yakamashii desu ga, Bankūbā wa shizuka desu. Tokyo is noisy, but Vancouver is quiet.

Nyūyōku wa shizuka ja arimasen ga, Washinton wa shizuka desu. New York is not quiet, but Washington is.

LESSON XI

Nihonjin wa ohashi de tabemasu. Japanese eat with chopsticks.

Kanadajin wa nan de tabemasu ka? What do Canadians eat with?

Anata wa osaji de kōhī ya kōcha o nomimasu ka? Do you drink coffee, tea, etc. with a spoon?

Iie, osaji de kōhī ya kōcha o nomi- No, I do not drink coffee, tea, etc.

masen.
Enpitsu de tegami o kakimasu ka?
Iie, enpitsu de kakimasen. Pen de kakimasu.
Anata wa Eigo o hanashimasu ka?
Hai, hanashimasu.
Furansugo mo hanashimasu ka?
Hai, Furansugo mo hanashimasu.
Watakushitachi wa me de nani o shimasu ka?
Me de mimasu.
Mimi de nani o shimasu ka?
Mimi de kikimasu.
Kuchi de nani o shimasu ka?
Kuchi de hanashimasu.
Hana de nani o shimasu ka?
Hana de nioi o kagimasu.
Te de nani o shimasu ka?
Iroiro no mono o mochimasu.
Ashi de arukimasu ne.
Kanadajin ya Amerikajin wa Eigo o hanashimasu keredomo, Supeinjin ya Aruzenchinjin wa Supeingo o hanashimasu.

with a spoon.
Do you write letters in pencil?
No, I do not write them in pencil.
I write them in ink.
Do you speak English?
Yes, I do.
Do you speak French too?
Yes, I speak French too.
What do we do with our eyes?

We see with our eyes.
What do we do with our ears?
We hear with our ears.
What do we do with our mouths?
We speak with our mouths.
What do we do with our noses?
We smell with our noses.
What do we do with our hands?
We hold various things with them.
We walk with our legs, don't we?
Canadians, Americans, etc., speak English, but Spaniards, Argentines, etc., speak Spanish.

LESSON XII

Anatagata wa kono gakkō de nani o naraimasu ka?

What do you study at this school?

Watakushitachi wa kono gakkō de Nihongo o naraimasu.

We study Japanese at this school.

Anata wa kono heya de tabemasu ka?

Do you eat in this room?

Iie, kono heya de tabemasen.

No, I do not eat in this room.

Horando-san wa anatagata ni Nihongo o oshiemasu ka?

Does Mr. Holland teach you Japanese?

Horando-san wa watakushitachi ni Nihongo o oshiemasen.

Mr. Holland does not teach us Japanese.

Anata wa tomodachi ni tegami o kakimasu ka?

Do you write letters to your friends?

Hai, tokidoki kakimasu.

Yes, I sometimes do.

Anata wa Furansugo ga wakarimasu ka?

Do you understand French?

Ano kata wa Nihongo ga yoku wakarimasu.

He understands Japanese well.

Anatagata wa Nihongo ga sukoshi wakarimasu.

You understand Japanese a little.

LESSON XIII

Watakushi wa nani o shimashita ka?	What did I do?
Anata wa anata no namae o kakimashita.	You wrote your name.
Nan de kakimashita ka?	What did I write with?
Enpitsu de kakimashita.	You wrote with a pencil.
Anata wa kinō Bikutoria e ikimashita ka?	Did you go to Victoria yesterday?
Iie, ikimasen deshita.	No, I did not.
Watakushi wa ima doa o akemashita ka?	Did I open the door just now?
Iie, akemasen deshita. Doa o shimemashita.	No, you did not. You shut it.

LESSON XIV

Kanada wa Nihon yori ōkii desu.	Canada is larger than Japan.
Bankūbā wa Honoruru yori samui desu ka?	Is Vancouver colder than Honolulu?
Hai, Bankūbā wa Honoruru yori samui desu.	Yes, Vancouver is colder than Honolulu.
Jidōsha wa jitensha yori takai desu ka?	Is an automobile more expensive than a bicycle?
Tōkyō to Yokohama to, dotchi ga ōkii desu ka?	Which is larger, Tokyo or Yokohama?
Tōkyō wa Yokohama yori ōkii desu.	Tokyo is larger than Yokohama.
Tōkyō no hō ga ōkii desu.	Tokyo is larger.
Ringo to banana to, dotchi ga yasui desu ka?	Which is cheaper, an apple or a banana?
Ringo wa banana yori yasui desu.	An apple is cheaper than a banana.
Ringo no hō ga yasui desu.	An apple is cheaper.
Sukiyaki to tenpura to, dotchi ga suki desu ka?	Which do you like better, 'sukiyaki' or 'tenpura'?
Tenpura no hō ga suki desu.	I like 'tenpura' better.

LESSON XV

Jibiki to zasshi to shinbun to, dore ga ichiban atsui desu ka?	Which is the thickest, a dictionary, a magazine or a newspaper?
Jibiki ga ichiban atsui desu.	A dictionary is the thickest.

Nihongo to Supeingo to Furansugo to, dore ga ichiban muzukashii desu ka?

Which is the most difficult, Japanese, Spanish or French?

Nihongo ga ichiban muzukashii desu.

Japanese is the most difficult.

Hikōki to jidōsha to kisha to, dore ga ichiban hayai desu ka?

Which is the fastest, an airplane, a car or a train?

Hikōki ga ichiban hayai desu.

An airplane is the fastest.

Gyūniku to butaniku to toriniku to, dore ga ichiban oishii desu ka?

Which is the most delicious, beef, pork or chicken?

Gyūniku ga ichiban oishii desu.

Beef is the most delicious.

LESSON XVI

Tsukue no ue ni akai kami ga sanmai arimasu.

There are three sheets of red paper on the desk.

Kiiroi kami mo sanmai arimasu.

There are three sheets of yellow paper too.

Minna de nanmai arimasu ka?

How many sheets of paper are there in all?

Rokumai arimasu.

There are six sheets of paper.

Hako no naka ni tabako ga nanbon arimasu ka?

How many cigarettes are there in the pack?

Jūnihon arimasu.

There are twelve cigarettes.

Anata wa kyō tabako o nanbon nomimashita ka?

How many cigarettes did you smoke today?

Gohon nomimashita.

I smoked five cigarettes.

Kaban no naka ni hon ga nansatsu arimasu ka?

How many books are there in the suitcase?

Nisatsu arimasu.

There are two books.

Isu no shita ni chairo no kutsu ga issoku arimasu.

There is a pair of brown shoes under the chair.

Maiasa kōhī o nanbai nomimasu ka?

How many cups of coffee do you drink every morning?

LESSON XVII

Kyōto wa Tōkyō gurai ōkii desu ka?

Is Kyoto as large as Tokyo?

Iie, Kyōto wa Tōkyō hodo ōkiku arimasen.

No, Kyoto is not as large as Tokyo.

Neko wa inu gurai hayaku hashirimasu ka?

Does a cat run as fast as a dog?

Iie, neko wa inu hodo hayaku ha-

No, a cat does not run as fast as

shirimasen.

Kyō wa kinō gurai suzushii desu ka?

Is today as cool as yesterday?

Hai, kyō wa kinō gurai suzushii desu.

Yes, today is as cool as yesterday.

Sukī wa sukēto gurai yasashii desu ka?

Is skiing as easy as skating?

Iie, sukī wa sukēto hodo yasashiku arimasen.

No, skiing is not as easy as skating.

LESSON XVIII

Kono heya ni hito ga nannin imasu ka?

How many persons are there in this room?

Hachinin imasu.

There are eight persons.

Otona ga gonin, kodomo ga sannin imasu.

There are five grown-ups, and three children.

Otona wa minna otoko no hito desu ka?

Are all the grown-ups men?

Iie, futari wa otoko no hito de, sannin wa onna no hito desu.

No, two of them are men and three of them are women.

Kodomo wa minna onna no ko desu ka?

Are all the children girls?

Iie, hitori wa otoko no ko de, futari wa onna no ko desu.

No, one of them is a boy and two of them are girls.

A'.achan wa imasen ka?

Aren't there any babies?

Hai, imasen.

No, there are not.

Ichiban chiisai otoko no ko wa ikutsu gurai desu ka?

About how old is the smallest boy?

Sō desu nē, mittsu gurai desu.

Well, he is about three years old.

Koko ni Nihonjin ga imasu ka?

Are there any Japanese here?

Hai, hitori imasu.

Yes, there is one Japanese.

Kanadajin wa nannin imasu ka?

How many Canadians are there in here? (As for Canadians, how many are there?)

LESSON XIX

Otoko no hito wa nani o shite imasu ka?

What is the man doing?

Hataraite imasu.

He is working.

Onna no hito mo hataraite imasu ka?

Is the woman working too?

Iie, hataraite imasen. Yasunde
imasu.
Onna no hito wa nani o kite imasu
ka?
'Kimono' o kite imasu.
Kodomo wa nani o kite imasu ka?
Yōfuku o kite imasu.
Jōnzu-san wa nani o yonde imasu
ka?
Nihon no shinbun o yonde imasu.

Anata wa tatte imasu ka, kakete
imasu ka?
Anatagata wa ima nani o shite
imasu ka?
Nihongo o naratte imasu.
Watakushi wa hanashite imasu ga,
anatagata wa kiite imasu.
Anata wa hidari no te ni nani o
motte imasu ka?
Hon o motte imasu.
Dewa, migi no te ni nani o motte
imasu ka?
Nannimo motte imasen.
Anata wa uwagi o kite imasu ka?
Iie, kite imasen.
Naze desu ka?
Atsui kara desu.
Howaito-san wa donna iro no ku-
tsu o haite imasu ka?
Shiroi kutsu o haite imasu.
Ikeda-san to okusan wa hiroi michi
o aruite imasu.
Ikeda-san wa nezumiiro-no uwagi
o kite, chairo-no zubon o haite,
kuroi kutsu o haite imasu.
Ikeda-san no okusan wa momoiro-
no kimono o kite, shiroi zōri o
haite imasu.
Watakushi wa nani o shite ima-
shita ka?
Zasshi o yonde imashita.
Anata wa hanashite imashita ka?
Iie, hanashite imasen deshita. Kiite
imashita.

No, she is not. She is resting.

What is the woman wearing?

She is wearing 'kimono'.
What is the child wearing?
He is wearing Western clothes.
What is Mr. Jones reading?

He is reading a Japanese newspaper.
Are you standing, or seated?

What are you doing now?

We are studying Japanese.
I am speaking, but (and) you are
listening.
What are you holding in your left
hand?
I am holding a book.
What are you holding in your right
hand, then?
I am holding nothing.
Are you wearing your coat?
No, I am not.
Why not?
Because it is hot.
What color shoes is Mr. White
wearing?
He is wearing white shoes.
Mr. Ikeda and his wife are walk-
ing along the wide road.
Mr. Ikeda is wearing a grey coat,
brown pants, and black shoes.

Mrs. Ikeda is wearing pink 'kimono' and white sandals.

What was I doing?

You were reading a magazine.
Were you talking?
No, I was not. I was listening.

LESSON XX

Ima nanji desu ka?	What time is it now?
Rokuji-han desu.	It is 6:30.
Anata wa maiasa nanji ni okimasu ka?	What time do you get up every morning?
Taitei shichiji goro okimasu.	I generally get up about 7.
Nanji ni asagohan o tabemasu ka?	What time do you eat breakfast?
Ohirugohan wa nanji desu ka?	What time is your lunch?
Jūniji ka jūniji-han goro desu.	It is about 12 or 12:30.
Kanadajin wa bangohan o osoku tabemasu ka?	Do Canadians eat supper late?
Hai, Kanadajin wa Amerikajin yori osoku tabemasu.	Yes, they eat later than Americans.
Anata wa kinō no ban nanji ni yasumimashita ka?	What time did you go to bed last night?
Jūji jūgofun mae goro yasumimashita.	I went to bed about 9:45 p.m.
Asa rokuji ni okite, ban jūji ni yasumimasu.	I wake up at 6 a.m., and go to bed at 10 p.m.
Kono kurasu wa nanji ni hajimarimasu ka?	What time does this class begin?
Hachiji gofun ni hajimarimasu.	It begins at 8:05.
Nanji ni owarimasu ka?	What time does it end?
Kuji gofun ni owarimasu.	It ends at 9:05.
Anata no tokei wa atte imasu ka?	Is your watch correct?
Sanpun gurai susunde imasu.	It is about three minutes fast.
Watakushi no tokei wa gofun okurete imasu.	My watch is five minutes slow.
Anata wa nanjikan nemasu ka?	How many hours do you sleep?
Rokujikan gurai desu.	About six hours.

LESSON XXI

Kyō wa naniyōbi desu ka?	What day of the week is it today?
Getsuyōbi desu.	It is Monday.
Anata wa doyōbi ni gakkō e kimasu ka?	Do you come to school on Saturdays?
Kanadajin wa maishū kinyōbi ni sakana o tabemasu ka?	Do Canadians eat fish every Friday?
Hai, aru hito wa tabemasu.	Yes, some people do.
Kinō wa nichiyōbi deshita ka?	Was yesterday Sunday?
Hai, nichiyōbi deshita.	Yes, it was.
Ashita wa suiyōbi desu ka, mokuyōbi desu ka?	Is tomorrow Wednesday or Thursday?

Suiyōbi demo mokuyōbi demo arimasen. Kayōbi desu.	It is neither Wednesday nor Thursday. It is Tuesday.
Anata wa nichiyōbi ni kyōkai e ikimasu ka?	Do you go to church on Sundays?
Watakushitachi wa Kurisumasu ni nishūkan yasumimasu.	We have a two-week vacation at Christmas.
Maishū nanjikan Nihongo o benkyō-shimasu ka?	How many hours do you study Japanese a week?
Maishū gojikan benkyō-shimasu.	We study it five hours a week.
Ototoi wa warui tenki deshita ne.	It was bad weather the day before yesterday, wasn't it?
Ame ga asa kara yūgata made furimashita.	It rained from morning till early evening.
Watakushi wa asatte Shiatoru e ikimasu.	I am going to Seattle the day after tomorrow.

LESSON XXII

Sangatsu, shigatsu, gogatsu wa haru de, rokugatsu, shichigatsu, hachigatsu wa natsu desu.	March, April and May are the spring months, and June, July and August are the summer months.
Kugatsu, jūgatsu, jūichigatsu wa aki de, jūnigatsu, ichigatsu, nigatsu wa fuyu desu.	September, October and November are the autumn months, and December, January and February are the winter months.
Haru wa atatakakute, natsu wa atsui desu.	Spring is warm and summer is hot.
Aki wa suzushikute, fuyu wa samui desu.	Autumn is cool and winter is cold.
Sakura wa nangatsu ni saku deshō ka?	In what month do the cherryblossoms come out?
Sangatsu no owari ka shigatsu no hajime ni sakimasu.	They come out at the end of March or the beginning of April.
Yuki wa nangatsu ni furimasu ka?	In what month does it snow?
Jūnigatsu no nakagoro ni furu deshō.	It will snow about the middle of December.
Ame wa nigatsu ni furu deshō ka?	Will it rain in February?
Iie, furanai deshō.	No, it won't.
Anata wa rainen Tōkyō e ikimasu ka?	Are you going to Tokyo next year?
Kotoshi wa nannen desu ka?	What year is this?
Sen kyūhyaku rokujūsan-nen desu.	It is 1963.
Buraun-san wa kyonen Bankūbā ni imashita ka?	Was Mr. Brown in Vancouver last year?
Iie, imasen deshita.	No, he was not.
Kongetsu wa nangatsu desu ka?	What month is this?

Jūgatsu desu.	It is October.
Dewa, raigetsu wa jūichigatsu desu ne.	Next month is November then, isn't it?
Sengetsu wa kugatsu deshita.	Last month was September.
Gakusei wa daigaku de nannen benkyō-shimasu ka?	How many years do students study at college?
Yonen benkyō-shimasu.	They study four years.
Anatagata wa nankagetsu Nihongo o naratte imasu ka?	How many months have you been studying Japanese?
Nikagetsu gurai naratte imasu.	We have been studying it about two months.

LESSON XXIII

Kyō wa nannichi desu ka?	What day of the month is it to-day?
Mikka desu.	It is the 3rd.
Dewa, ashita wa itsuka desu nē.	Tomorrow is the 5th then, isn't it?
Iie, chigaimasu. Ashita wa yokka desu.	No, you are wrong. Tomorrow is the 4th.
Ototoi wa futsuka deshita ka?	Was the day before yesterday the 2nd?
Iie, tsuitachi deshita.	No, it was the 1st.
Tōkyō no aru mise wa maigetsu tsuitachi to jūgonichi ni yasumimasu.	Some stores in Tokyo are closed on the 1st and the 15th every month.
Anata no tanjōbi wa itsu desu ka?	When is your birthday?
Nigatsu jūichinichi desu.	It is February 11.
Kurisumasu wa itsu desu ka?	When is Christmas?
Jūnigatsu nijūgonichi desu.	It is December 25.

LESSON XXIV

Bankūbā wa itsu atsuku narimasu ka?	When does it become hot in Vancouver?
Shichigatsu ni sukoshi atsuku narimasu.	It becomes a little hot in July.
Asa nanji goro akaruku narimasu ka?	About what time does it become bright in the morning?
Goji goro akaruku narimasu.	It becomes bright about 5.
Yūgata rokuji ni kuraku naru deshō ka?	Will it become dark at 6 p.m.?
Iie, kuraku naranai deshō.	No, it won't become dark.
Uisukī o nomu to, kao ga akaku narimasu ka?	If you drink whisky, does your face become red?
Iie, chittomo akaku narimasen.	No, it does not become red at all.

Mainichi hanasu to, jōzu ni narimasu ka?	If one speaks it every day, will he become good at it?
Jōzu ni naru to omoimasu.	I think he will.
Nihongo wa muzukashii to omoimasu ka?	Do you think Japanese is difficult?
Ame ga furu to, samuku narimasu ka, atsuku narimasu ka?	If (when) it rains, does it become cold or hot?
Ame ga furu to, samuku narimasu.	If (when) it rains, it becomes cold.
Kaze ga fuku to, hokori ga tachimasu.	If (when) it blows, dust rises.
Kono hankachi o arau to, kirei ni naru to omoimasu ka?	Do you think that if I wash this handkerchief, it will become clean?
Kirei ni naranai to omoimasu.	I do not think it will become clean.
Aruku to, jōbu ni narimasu ne.	If we walk, we become healthy, don't we?

LESSON XXV

Shūmatsu ni dokoka e ikitai desu ka?	Do you want to go somewhere over the weekend?
Ongakukai e ikitai desu. Ii ongaku o kikitai desu kara.	I would like to go to a concert because I would like to listen to good music.
Kyō no gogo eiga o mitai desu ka?	Do you want to go to the movies this afternoon?
Iie, mitaku arimasen. Kutabiremashita kara.	No, I do not want to because I am tired.
Ima kōhī o nomitai desu ka?	Would you like to drink coffee now?
Hai, nomitai desu. Nodo ga kawakimashita kara.	Yes, I would because I am thirsty.
Nanika tabetai desu ka?	Do you want to eat something?
Iie, nannimo tabetaku arimasen. Onaka ga suite imasen.	No, I do not want to eat anything. I am not hungry.
Tegami o kakitai toki ni, nani ga irimasu ka?	When one wants to write a letter, what does he need?
Kami to fūtō to pen ga irimasu.	He needs paper, an envelope, and ink.
Kukkī o tsukuritai toki ni, batā ga irimasu ka?	When one wants to make cookies, does she need butter?
Kinō issho-ni ikitai deshita ka?	Did you want to go with me yesterday?
Iie, ikitaku arimasen deshita.	No, I did not.

LESSON XXVI

Anata wa Eigo o hanasu koto ga dekimasu ka? — Can you speak English?

Hai, dekimasu. — Yes, I can.

Gurīku-san wa Nihongo o hanasu koto ga dekimasu ka? — Can Mr. Greek speak Japanese?

Iie, dekimasen. — No, he cannot.

Ano kata wa Nihon no shinbun o yomu koto ga dekimasu ka? — Can he read a Japanese newspaper?

Dekiru ka dō ka shirimasen. — I do not know whether he can or not.

Bikutoria e ichijikan de iku koto ga dekimasu ka? — Can we go to Victoria in an hour?

Iie, dekinai deshō. — No, perhaps we cannot.

Ohashi de taberu koto ga dekimasu ka? — Can you eat with chopsticks?

Hai, heta desu ga, dekimasu. — Yes, I can. I am poor (at it), though.

Anata wa Supeingo ga hanasemasu ka? — Can you speak Spanish?

Hai, sukoshi hanasemasu. — Yes, I can speak it a little.

Jōnzu-san wa 'kanji' ga kakemasu ka? — Can Mr. Jones write 'kanji'?

Kakeru to omoimasu. — I think he can.

Mō sukoshi hayaku arukemasen ka? — Can't you walk a little faster?

Iie, arukemasu. — Yes, I can.

Kono pan wa taberaremasu ka? — Is this bread edible?

Iie, katakute taberaremasen. — No, it is stale and is not edible.

Sono gaitō wa chiisakute, kiraremasen. — That overcoat is so small I cannot wear.

LESSON XXVII

Kinō kita tegami — a letter which came yesterday

Kodomo ga yomu hon — books which children read

Soko ni tatte iru hito — the person who is standing there

Tsukue no ue ni aru hon wa donata no desu ka? — Whose is the book which is on the desk?

Tsukue no ue ni aru hon wa watakushi no desu. — The book which is on the desk is mine.

Takami-san ga yonde iru shinbun wa nan to iu namae desu ka? — What is the name of the newspaper which Mr. Takami is reading?

'Asahi' to iu namae desu. — It is the 'Asahi'.

Anata ga tsukatte iru mannenhitsu wa Kanada-sei desu ka?
Is the fountain-pen which you are using of Canadian make?

Hai, sō desu.
Yes, it is.

Senshū mita eiga wa dō deshita ka?
How was the movie which you saw last week?

Totemo ii deshita.
It was very good.

Asuko ni iru hito wa dare desu ka?
Who is that person over there?

Asuko ni iru hito wa watakushi no furui tomodachi de, Kūpā to iu hito desu.
He is a friend of mine and his name is Cooper.

Yogoreta waishatsu o kite pātī e ikitai desu ka?
Do you wish to go to a party with a dirty shirt on?

Iie, ikitaku arimasen.
No, I do not.

Futotte iru hito wa natsu atsui desu ka?
Is a stout person hot in summer?

Tabun atsui deshō. Shikashi, yasete iru hito wa fuyu samui sō desu.
Perhaps he is hot. However, a skinny person is cold in winter, I understand.

Hareta hi to kumotta hi to, dotchi ga gorufu ni ii desu ka?
Which is better for golfing, a fine day or a cloudy day?

Hareta hi no hō ga ii desu.
A fine day is better.

Anata no totta shashin o misete kudasai.
Please show me the picture you took.

LESSON XXVIII

Nante kawaii deshō!
How cute she is!

Kono sūpu wa nante karai deshō!
How salty this soup is!

Kinō wa nante samukatta deshō!
How cold it was yesterday!

Nante ōkiku natta deshō!
How big it has become!

Nante kirei ni natta deshō!
How beautiful she has become!

Nante kirei-na hana deshō!
What a pretty flower it is!

Nante takai ki deshō!
What a tall tree it is!

LESSON XXIX

Bin no yoko ni nani ga kaite arimasu ka?
What is written on the side of the bottle?

Eigo to Nihongo ga kaite arimasu.
English and Japanese are written.

Kono chiisana hako no naka ni nani ga irete arimasu ka?
What is put in this small box?

Matchi ga irete arimasu.
Matches are put in it.

Anata no ōkina kaban wa doko ni oite arimasu ka?
Where is your big suitcase placed?

Yuka no ue ni oite arimasu.   It is placed on the floor.

Doa wa akete arimasu ka, shimete arimasu ka?   Is the door open or closed?

Ehagaki ni kitte ga hatte arimasu ka?   Is a stamp affixed to a picture postcard?

Iie, hatte arimasen.   No, it is not.

Kabe ni nani ga kakete arimasu ka?   What is hung up on the wall?

E ga kakete arimasu.   A picture is hung up.

LESSON XXX

Mado o akete mo ii desu ka?   May I open the window?

Hai, akete mo ii desu.   Yes, you may.

Enpitsu de tegami o kaite mo ii desu ka?   May I write a letter in pencil?

Iie, kaite wa ikemasen.   No, you must not.

Kyōshitsu de bīru o nonde mo ii desu ka?   May we drink beer in the classroom?

Iie, nonde wa ikemasen.   No, you must not.

Arukinagara ringo o tabete mo ii desu ka?   May one eat an apple while walking?

Iie, arukinagara ringo o tabete wa ikemasen.   No, he must not eat an apple while walking.

Uwagi o nuide mo ii desu ka?   May I take off my coat?

Hai, nuide mo ii desu.   Yes, you may.

Osake o nonde jidōsha o unten-shite wa ikemasen ka?   Shouldn't one drive a car under the influence of liquor?

Hai, unten-shite wa ikemasen. Abunai kamo shiremasen.   No, he should not. It may be dangerous.

LESSON XXXI

Kusuri o nomeba, byōki wa naorimasu ka?   Will you be cured of your sickness, if you take medicine?

Hai, taitei naorimasu.   Yes, I am generally cured.

Yukkuri hanaseba, wakarimasu ka?   Do you understand, if I talk slowly?

Hai, wakarimasu.   Yes, I do.

Takusan tabereba, nemuku narimasu ka?   Do you become sleepy, if you eat a lot?

Hai, tokidoki nemuku narimasu.   Yes, I sometimes do.

Kyō kono tegami o daseba, asatte Otawa ni tsukimasu ka?   If I mail this letter now, will it get to Ottawa the day after tomorrow?

Hai, tsuku deshō.
Ame ga fureba, uchi ni imasu ka?

Hai, iru tsumori desu.
Ima ikeba, sanji no basu ni ma ni aimasu ka?
Hai, ma ni aimasu.
Yoku benkyō-sureba, jōzu ni naremasu ka?
Hai, mochiron jōzu ni naremasu yo.
Yasukereba, kaitai desu ka?

Hai, kaitai desu.
Atsukereba, dō shimasu ka?
Atsukereba, mado ya doa o akemasu.
Okane ga nakereba, hairemasen ka?
Hai, hairemasen.
Akarukereba, miemasu ga, kurakereba, miemasen.
Chikakereba, kikoemasu ga, tōkereba, kikoemasen.
Tenki ga warukereba, ikanaide kudasai.
Tōkereba, kuruma ka basu de iku hō ga ii deshō.
Kirai nara, tabenaide kudasai.

Jōbu nara, kusuri wa irimasen.

Yes, it will.
If it rains, are you going to stay at home?
Yes, I intend to stay at home.
If you go now, will you be in time for the 3 o'clock bus?
Yes, I will.
Can I become good at it, if I work hard?
Yes, of course you can.

Do you want to buy it, if it is cheap?
Yes, I do.
What will you do, if it is hot?
If it is hot, I will open the windows and doors.
Can't I enter, if I have no money?

No, you cannot.
If it is bright, we can see, but if it is dark, we cannot see.
If it is near, we can hear, but if it is far away, we cannot hear.
If it is bad weather, please do not go.
If it is far, you had better go by car or by bus.
If you do not like it, please do not eat it.
If you are in good shape, you do not need any medicine.

LESSON XXXII

Ame ga fureba, gakkō e kimasen ka?
Iie, ame ga futte mo, kimasu.
Kusuri o nomeba, byōki wa naorimasu ka?
Iie, aru byōki wa kusuri o nonde mo, naorimasen.

Otaku wa koko kara tōi desu ka?
Iie, tōku arimasen. Aruite mo, nisan-pun shika kakarimasen.

Won't you come to school, if it rains?
Yes, I will come, even if it rains.
Will you be cured of your sickness, if you take medicine?
No, you won't be cured of some sicknesses, even if you take medicine.
Is your home far from here?
No, it is not. Even if you walk, it will take only two or three minutes.

Samukereba, mado o shimete nete mo ii desu ka?
Iie, samukute mo, mado o akete neru hō ga ii deshō.
Ha ga itakereba, jimusho e ikimasen ka?
Iie, ha ga itakute mo, jimusho e ikimasu.

May we sleep with the windows closed, if it is cold?
No, we had better sleep with the windows open, even if it is cold.
Won't you go to the office, if you have a toothache?
Yes, I will go to the office, even if I have a toothache.

LESSON XXXIII

Seito wa benkyō-shinakereba ikemasen ka?
Hai, benkyō-shinakereba ikemasen.
Anata wa nanji made ni koko e konakereba ikemasen ka?
Kuji made ni konakereba ikemasen.
Kanada no kōtōgakkō no seito wa mainichi gakkō e ikanakereba narimasen ka?
Doyō to nichiyō no hoka wa mainichi ikanakereba narimasen.
Watakushitachi wa shinbun o yomanakereba narimasen ka?
Iie, yomanakute mo ii desu ga, yomu hō ga ii desu.
Gyūnyū o nomanakereba narimasen ka?
Hai, nomanakereba narimasen. Gyūnyū wa karada ni ii desu kara.
Hagaki ni kitte o haranakereba ikemasen ka?
Iie, haranakute mo ii desu. Kitte wa insatsu-shite arimasu.
Kōen ni hairu no ni kippu o kawanakereba narimasen ka?
Iie, kawanakute mo ii desu.

Do pupils have to study?
Yes, they have to study.
By what time must you come here?
I must come here by 9.
Do the high school students in Canada have to go to school every day?
They have to go every day except Saturdays and Sundays.
Do we have to read a newspaper?
No, we do not have to read, but we had better read.
Must we drink milk?
Yes, we must because it is good for us.
Must we affix a stamp to a post-card?
No, we do not need to. A stamp is printed on it.
Must we buy a ticket in order to enter a park?
No, we do not need to.

LESSON XXXIV

Kodomo wa tokidoki oya ni shikararemasu ka?
Hai, shikararemasu. Itazura o shimasu kara.

Do children sometimes get scolded by their parents?
Yes, they do because they do mischief.

Rinkān wa dare ni utaremashita ka?

By whom was Lincoln shot?

Būsu to iu hito ni utaremashita.

He was shot by a man called Booth.

Donna seito ga sensei ni homeraremasu ka?

What kind of pupils get praised by their teachers?

Yoku benkyō-suru seito ga homeraremasu.

Those pupils who work hard do.

Shōsetsuka no Mōmu wa Kanadajin ni shirarete imasu ka?

Is Maughaum, the novelist, known to Canadians?

Hai, shirarete iru to omoimasu.

Yes, I think he is.

Okyaku wa taitei daidokoro e tōsaremasu ka?

Is a guest usually shown into the kitchen?

Iie, daidokoro e tōsaremasen. Kyakuma e tōsaremasu.

No, he is not. He will be shown into the drawing room.

Anata wa saifu o torareta koto ga arimasu ka?

Have you ever been robbed of your purse?

Iie, mada torareta koto ga arimasen.

No, I have not.

Anata wa sensei ni nandomo machigai o naosaremasu ka?

Do you get your mistakes corrected by your teacher many times?

Hai, nandomo naosarete, hazukashii desu.

Yes, I do and I am ashamed of it.

Tomodachi ni korarete, benkyō dekinai koto ga arimasu ka?

Do your friends sometimes come on you and you cannot study?

Hai, tama-ni arimasu.

Yes, they do once in a while.

Ame ni furarete, kasa ga nakereba, dō narimasu ka?

What will happen, if you are caught in the rain and if you do not have an umbrella with you?

Tabun nurete shimaimasu.

Perhaps I will be wet through.

LESSON XXXV

Anata wa jibun de kutsu o migakimasu ka?

Do you shine your shoes by yourself?

Iie, itsumo ototo ni migakasemasu.

No, I always make my younger brother shine them.

Oishasan wa byōnin ni bīru o nomasemasu ka?

Does a doctor allow a patient to drink beer?

Iie, nomasenai deshō.

No, he won't.

Kanada no shōgakkō de wa, sensei wa seito ni hon o yomasemasu ka?

Do grade school teachers make their pupils read books in Canada?

Sensei wa warui seito o tatasemasu ka?

Do teachers make bad pupils stand?

Anata wa tomodachi o matasemasu ka?

Do you keep your friends waiting?

Onna no tomodachi nara, kesshite matasemasen.

Mataseru to, okorimasu kara.

Okāsan wa akachan ni niku o tabesasemasu ka?
Tabesasenai deshō.
Donata ni kudamono ya yasai ya tamago o kawasemasu ka?
Kanai ni kawasemasu ga, jibun de kai ni iku koto mo arimasu.

If the friend is a girl, I never keep her waiting. (I never keep my girl friend waiting.)
The reason is that she will become angry, if I keep her waiting.
Will a mother make her baby eat meat?
Perhaps she won't.
Whom do you make buy fruits, vegetables, eggs, etc.?
I make my wife buy them, but I myself sometimes go and buy them.

LESSON XXXVI

Anata wa mise de matasaremasu ka?
Hai, mise ga konde ireba, matasaremasu.
Matasareru no wa suki desu ka, kirai desu ka?
Matasareru no wa kirai desu.
Kanada de wa, seito wa sensei ni hon o yomasaremasu ka?
Hai, seito wa sensei ni hon o yomasaremasu.
Resutoran de katai niku o tabesaserareta koto ga arimasu ka?
Hai, tabesaserareta koto ga arimasu.
Kodomo wa tabitabi otōsan ni heya o sōjisaseraremasu ka?
Hai, sōjisaseraremasu.

Are you kept waiting at a store?
Yes, I am kept waiting, if the store is crowded.
Do you like being kept waiting, or do you hate it?
I hate being kept waiting.
Are pupils made to read books by their teachers in Canada?
Yes, they are.

Have you ever been made to eat tough meat at a restaurant?
Yes, I have been made to eat it.

Are children often made to clean their rooms by their fathers?
Yes, they are.

LESSON XXXVII

Anata wa itsumo jibun de tegami o dashimasu ka?
Iie, itsumo imōto ni dashite moraimasu.
Tokei ga kowaretara, dō shimasu ka?

Do you always mail letters by yourself?
No, I always have them mailed by my younger sister.
What will you do, if your watch gets out of order?

Tokeiya e motte itte, naoshite moraimasu.

Tokoya de hige o sotte moraimasu ka?

Iie, sotte moraimasen. Kami dake katte moraimasu.

Okāsan no tanjōbi ni nani o katte agetai desu ka?

Shinju no yubiwa o katte agetai to omoimasu.

Tomodachi ga komatte iru toki ni, tasukete agemasu ka?

Hai, dekiru dake tasukete agemasu.

Okāsan wa mainichi oishii mono o koshiraete kudasaimasu ka?

Hai, hotondo mainichi koshiraete kudasaimasu.

Anata wa mise de appuru-pai o kaimasu ka?

Iie, kanai ga tsukutte kuremasu kara, metta-ni kaimasen.

I will take it to a watch-maker's and get it fixed.

Do you get a shave at a barber shop?

No, I do not. I get only a haircut.

What do you want to buy for your mother on her birthday?

I would like to buy a pearl ring for her.

Will you help your friends when they are in trouble?

Yes, I will help them as much as I can.

Does your mother make delicious things for you every day?

Yes, she makes them for me almost every day.

Do you buy apple-pies at a store?

No, I seldom do because my wife makes them for me.

LESSON XXXVIII

"Mado o akete kudasai." to iimashita.

Mado o akeru yō ni iimashita.

"Namae to jūsho o kaite kudasai." to iimasu.

Namae to jūsho o kaku yō ni iimasu.

"Ōkii koe de hanasanaide kudasai." to itte kudasai.

Ōkii koe de hanasanai yō ni itte kudasai.

Oishasan wa tabako o suu yō ni osshaimasu ka, suwanai yō ni osshaimasu ka?

Tabun suwanai yō ni ossharu deshō.

Nanji ni kuru yō ni iimashō ka?

Goji ni kuru yō ni itte kudasai.

He said, "Please open the window."

He told me to open the window.

He says, "Please write your name and address."

He tells me to write my name and address.

Please say to them, "Please do not talk in a loud voice."

Please tell them not to talk in a loud voice.

Will a doctor tell you to smoke or not to smoke?

Perhaps he will tell me not to smoke.

What time shall I tell him to come?

Please tell him to come at 5.

ENGLISH-JAPANESE TRANSLATION EXERCISES
(PART ONE)

LESSON I

1. What is that over there?
2. Is this a desk or a chair?
3. That is a magazine too.
4. This is not a book either.
5. Isn't that over there a sheet of paper?

LESSON II

1. Who is she?
2. Mr. Cook is an American.
3. Are you a student too?
4. I am not a teacher either.
5. Is he an American or an Englishman?
6. Isn't Mr. Asai a Japanese?

LESSON III

1. Is this a big box or a small box?
2. That over there is not a sheet of white paper either.
3. That is a red pencil too.
4. Isn't this a long pencil?
5. Isn't that over there a small desk?

LESSON IV

1. Are you cold too?
2. Is this suitcase black or white?
3. San Francisco is not hot.

4. Isn't that magazine over there expensive?
5. Tokyo is not cold either.
6. That blue box is not cheap.
7. Isn't Honolulu hot?

LESSON V

1. What color is your coat?
2. Are his trousers red too?
3. My black shoes are not small.
4. Isn't your fountain pen blue?
5. Mr. Brown's hat is not black either.
6. Your briefcase is not white, is it?
7. This magazine is big, isn't it?

LESSON VI

1. Whose is this short pencil?
2. Is that book over there yours or mine?
3. Is this big dictionary Mr. Higashi's or Mr. Nishi's?
4. Isn't that small watch hers?
5. These black shoes are not mine either.
6. Whose briefcase is this?

LESSON VII

1. Miss Brown is American and Miss Reed is French.
2. Whose are those big books and long pencils over there?
3. This yellow pencil is mine and that black pencil is yours.
4. Aren't these desks and chairs his?
5. This red book and that yellow book are not Mr. List's either.

LESSON VIII

1. Where is your small dictionary?
2. My books and pencils are in this big suitcase.
3. Is his magazine on your desk?
4. Isn't my white box under the chair?
5. His house is not in front of the school.
6. Are your books in the briefcase or on the desk?
7. Her blue shoes are behind that box over there.

LESSON IX

1. How many doors and windows are there in your room?
2. There is nothing in my pocket.
3. There are two desks and three chairs here.
4. What is over there?
5. How many big newspapers are there in Japan?

LESSON X

1. There are seven white flowers and nine red flowers in this beautiful vase.
2. Are there many universities in California?
3. Your shoes are expensive, but mine are cheap.
4. These yellow flowers are not beautiful either.
5. Tokyo is not quiet, but Kyoto is.

LESSON XI

1. What do you eat with?
2. I do not write letters in red pencil.
3. He speaks English and French.
4. Does he write 'kanji' too?
5. I drink coffee, tea, etc., but he drinks beer, whisky, etc.
6. Do you write letters in Japanese?

7. He holds various things with his left hand.

LESSON XII

1. What do we do in this room?
2. I do not speak German either.
3. What does Mr. Yoshida teach you here?
4. I sometimes write letters to my friends in Japanese.
5. Where do you eat?
6. She does not understand Chinese well.
7. He speaks English, French and Spanish a little.
8. Doesn't he sometimes speak to you in English?
9. What do you study at this university?

LESSON XIII

1. We did not go to school yesterday.
2. You walked, didn't you?
3. What did he write in pencil?
4. He went to your house just now.
5. Didn't you open this window?
6. I ate nothing.
7. Did you open the door, or close it?

LESSON XIV

1. My car is a little larger than yours.
2. Isn't Chicago colder than New York?
3. I eat more than you do.
4. Your handkerchief is whiter than hers, isn't it?
5. Does she know it better than I?
6. I prefer 'sukiyaki'.
7. Which do you like better, a big car or a small car?
8. He drank 'sake' more than I did.
9. Which is more expensive, a pencil or a fountain pen?

LESSON XV

1. Which is the largest, New York, Chicago or San Francisco?
2. I like beer best.
3. This thick dictionary is the most expensive.
4. She spoke English best.
5. Which do you speak best, English, French or German?
6. Isn't Japanese the most difficult?
7. Who is the tallest?
8. Which do you like best, beer, whisky or 'sake'?

LESSON XVI

1. There are two sheets of white paper and three sheets of red paper in my right pocket.
2. How many bottles of beer did you drink at Mr. Yoda's yesterday?
3. There were three big books and two small books in your suitcase.
4. There are twenty cigarettes in this pack.
5. She has three pairs of red shoes.
6. I drink two cups of hot coffee every morning.
7. There are two brown cars in front of my house.

LESSON XVII

1. This Japanese car is as expensive as an American car.
2. She speaks Japanese as well as I do.
3. She is not as pretty as you.
4. Yesterday was not as hot as today, was it?
5. Did you eat as much as he?
6. Japanese is not so easy as Spanish.
7. He runs as fast as I do.

LESSON XVIII

1. There were one American woman and two French men in the car.
2. How many girls went there?
3. How old is that biggest boy over there?
4. There were no grown-ups in the room.
5. How many Japanese are there in your school?
6. The smallest child is about 5 years old.
7. How many boys and girls did you see there?

LESSON XIX

1. Are you working, or resting?
2. They are studying Japanese at this school.
3. Why aren't you wearing your jacket now?
4. I was watching tv, but he was sleeping.
5. You are not holding a book in your left hand, are you?
6. Please write your name in ink.
7. That beautiful woman is wearing a pink dress and grey shoes.
8. Please come again.
9. Mrs. Power was not looking at anything.
10. What color are your socks?
11. He and his wife were reading newspapers in their big room.
12. Where were you waiting for me?
13. His coat is grey and his pants are brown.
14. We did not walk, because it was hot.
15. He and his children are wearing sandals, and are walking along the wide road.
16. This is cheap and good.
17. His girl friend is tall and pretty.

LESSON XX

1. I get up at 7:30 every morning.
2. What time did you go there?
3. He ate supper about 8 yesterday evening.
4. We go to bed about 11 every night.
5. He gets up at 7, eats breakfast at 8, and goes to school at 8:20.
6. School begins at 8:50 and ends at 3:15.
7. She went there at 6 and came back at 7.
8. How many hours do you work every day?
9. I did not sleep well last night.
10. They study Japanese for two hours every morning.

LESSON XXI

1. What day of the week was it yesterday?
2. We do not go to school on Saturdays and Sundays.
3. Some people eat fish every Friday.
4. She is neither American nor French.
5. I work from 9 to 5 on Mondays, Wednesdays and Thursdays.
6. Because it was fine weather, I walked from the church to my home.
7. The day before yesterday was not Tuesday.
8. The weather was very bad in the morning and it rained a lot at night.

LESSON XXII

1. He was in Tokyo for three months in 1965.
2. What month is this?
3. A friend of mine came and I did not go there.
4. We ate and drank in his room.
5. Honolulu is hot and Tokyo is cool now.

6. It was cold at the end of March, but was warm at the beginning of April.
7. The cherryblossoms won't come out in February, because it is cold.
8. Will it snow about the middle of next month?

LESSON XXIII

1. This store is closed on the 1st and the 20th.
2. My birthday is August 4.
3. On what day did he go to Yokohama?
4. She takes every Wednesday off.
5. What day of the month was it yesterday?
6. When did you hear that?

LESSON XXIV

1. Do you think it will become cold?
2. When it becomes warm, we open the windows.
3. If one listens to and speaks Japanese every day, he will become good at it, I think.
4. I do not think it will rain today.
5. Whenever it becomes cold, it snows.
6. If you read it fast, you won't understand it.

LESSON XXV

1. I did not want to go to the movies because I was tired.
2. What would you like to eat?
3. He was thirsty and wanted to drink water.
4. Do you need a dictionary when you read a Japanese newspaper?
5. She is in no mood to do so.
6. Did his wife want to buy a new car?

7. She wants to go to a concert tomorrow afternoon.
8. Where do you go when you want to listen to good music?

LESSON XXVI

1. This beef is so tough I cannot eat.
2. Can you commit these words to memory in a week?
3. I cannot run as fast as you.
4. He can speak English well because he was in New York for five years.
5. Your overcoat was small; so I could not wear it.
6. Can't you come tomorrow morning?
7. He did not tell me whether it was difficult or not.
8. We do not know whether she is coming to our party or not.
9. Do you think we can get there in twenty minutes?
10. I was so busy that I could not eat lunch; so I am really hungry.

LESSON XXVII

1. The thick and black dictionary which was on the desk belongs to his father.
2. Mr. and Mrs. Honda who are coming from Tokyo by plane tomorrow will stay here for a week.
3. How was the supper you had at the hotel?
4. They say Tokyo is noisier.
5. I would like to go there on a fine day.
6. Are there many people who do not smoke?
7. There are two students who are able to speak and write Japanese in this class.
8. Who is the lady seated next to you?
9. I understand he cannot read 'kanji'.
10. The old fountain pen which I was using does not belong to me.

11. Is the girl who was here a little while ago a friend of yours?
12. The American who is speaking fluent Japanese over there stayed in Japan for ten years.
13. Are there any books you would like to take to your home?
14. The man with whom I talked here yesterday had come from Toronto.
15. The camera with which I took this picture is made in Japan.

LESSON XXVIII

1. How good you have become at it!
2. What an expensive bicycle he has bought!
3. How big that American boy over there has grown!
4. What fine weather it is!
5. What a heavy drinker he is!
6. How windy it is!
7. How delicious the cake you baked this morning is!

LESSON XXIX

1. Nothing is written on this bottle.
2. No postage stamp was affixed to this picture post-card.
3. Where is your hat hung up?
4. Books, paper, pencils, etc. were placed on my desk.
5. What is put in your pocket?

LESSON XXX

1. You must not read a newspaper while eating supper.
2. She and I talked over coffee.
3. May I come about 10 tomorrow morning?
4. It may perhaps rain tonight.
5. His house may be a little bigger.

6. She may not know my name.
7. I may be able to lend it.
8. He may have forgotten his wallet.
9. You may walk, but you must not run.

LESSON XXXI

1. If it rains, I do not want to go.
2. If it is inexpensive and good, she may perhaps buy it.
3. Will he become good at it, if he speaks it every day?
4. Do you intend to play golf, if it is warm?
5. If we do not have money, we cannot enter.
6. Please do not wait, if I am late.
7. If you take this medicine and rest, you will be all right in a day or two.
8. He will follow you, if you speak slowly and clearly.
9. If you mail this letter in the morning, it will get there in the evening.
10. If you take off now, you may perhaps make the 5:30 train.
11. If you study Japanese for one more year, you will be able to read Japanese newspapers.
12. If you want to take a good look at it, you can take it to your room.
13. If it does not snow, I would like to go.
14. If it is not good, I won't buy it.
15. If you do not take this medicine, you won't be cured.
16. If you do not write him, he won't write you.
17. If you do not want to see it, you do not have to.

LESSON XXXII

1. Even if it is far away, I would like to walk.
2. Even if one can read it, one may perhaps not be able to write it.

3. Please come, even if it snows.
4. Only five or six persons showed up.
5. You had better wash it, even if it is not dirty.
6. Sometimes you may not be cured of your sickness, even if you take good medicine.
7. We had better not sleep with this large window open.
8. Even if I want to learn it, I cannot find a teacher.
9. It took only one hour and a half.
10. Even if you have a headache, you had better not stay away from school.
11. Even if you have only one dollar, you can eat nice supper here.

LESSON XXXIII

1. I had to finish this by noon today.
2. You will have to put this sweater on because it has become cold.
3. He may have to hurry.
4. You do not have to do so, if you do not want to.
5. I did not have to show you the map.
6. Nobody except you will like it.
7. It has to be white and thin.
8. By what time do you have to arrive at the station?
9. We may perhaps need a Japanese-English dictionary in order to read newspapers.
10. Do I have to remember what you said?

LESSON XXXIV

1. I have never been to New York.
2. Have you read the novel entitled "Yukiguni"?
3. He has never been praised by his teacher.
4. The novelist was not known to us Japanese.
5. His brother was caught in the rain and was wet.
6. I do not want to be seen by you because I am not dressed.

7. Have you finished brushing your teeth?
8. We get our mistakes corrected by our teacher many times every day.
9. The magazine called "Life" is being read by a great number of people.
10. I have forgotten it completely.
11. Have you ever got your watch stolen?

LESSON XXXV

1. Please do not keep me waiting too long.
2. We cannot let you do so.
3. There are cases in which it is windy in the fall.
4. Did your mother make you buy it?
5. I do not want to make you work, if you do not want to work,
6. I do not think your doctor will allow you to go to the office, because you have a high fever.
7. Two friends of mine came to have a chat last night.
8. He may perhaps make me continue the work.
9. She went shopping on the Ginza with her children.
10. There are occasions on which I get angry.
11. Her father will not allow me to come to see her.

LESSON XXXVI

1. I have never been made to study this hard.
2. What would you do, if you were kept waiting?
3. Do you wish to be made to open it?
4. It is difficult to eat with chopsticks.
5. I saw you go out of the room.
6. We may be made to walk.
7. It will be easier to read them than to write them.
8. Have you ever heard him speak Japanese?
9. I was compelled to do so by an old friend of mine.

10. It is not good to drive a car under the influence of liquor.
11. It may not be too difficult to translate Japanese into English.

LESSON XXXVII

1. Will you help me when I am in trouble?
2. I want you to clean it.
3. It often rains, but seldom snows.
4. Why don't you get your broken watch fixed?
5. Shall I do so for you now?
6. His five-year-old boy was kind enough to show me the way.
8. He may perhaps telephone her for me.

LESSON XXXVIII

1. Would you mind telling the man who is standing there to come in and wait?
2. He said, "Please walk fast."
3. I do not have to tell you not to smoke in this room, do I?
4. Who told you not to talk in a loud voice?
5. Her doctor advised her not to eat anything today and tomorrow.
6. You should not tell a small child to do such a difficult thing.
7. What time did you tell me to go?
8. She said, "Please do not scold me."
9. Father said, "I will be back about 6."
10. Please tell him to wait.

ENGLISH-JAPANESE TRANSLATION EXERCISES
(PART TWO)

LESSON I

1. We have only upper berths.
2. Express trains do not stop at small stations.
3. Nobody except Mr. Kimura came to the party yesterday.
4. If you do not have a large one, this small one will do.
5. A dining car is not attached to this train.
6. You had better send him a telegram before you get there.
7. I don't know whether or not he can write a letter in Japanese.
8. Please tell him that I came to see him this morning.

LESSON II

1. How long did it take you to make this?
2. I will come home by 3 at the latest.
3. These children play outdoors if it is fine weather.
4. They live next door to us.

LESSON III

1. She was kind enough to show me the book she had bought.
2. How about a cup of coffee?
3. I like neckties of a quiet color.
4. Did he find this to his taste?
5. It has become somewhat warmer, hasn't it?
6. She is always gaily dressed.
7. This is the same as mine, I think.
8. It cost me ten dollars, if I remember correctly.
9. Commodity prices are going up with the exception of socks.
10. This looks like my dictionary.
11. Please wrap it up because it is a gift.
12. Excuse me, but is this the way to the post office?
13. Unluckily it rained; so we could not go.

14. We are sold out of small ones.
15. I know no words to apologize for it.
16. Can I leave this with you for a day or two?
17. Here's one dollar change, sir.

LESSON IV

1. Come right in, please.
2. How long do you intend to stay?
3. Apparently he was tired. He turned in as soon as he ate supper.
4. Even a grade school pupil knows it.
5. I will come whenever it is convenient for you.
6. I hate to bother you, but could you open the door for me?
7. I will see to it that these letters are mailed tomorrow morning.
8. We want you to write your name, age, address, and occupation.
9. How often should I take this medicine?
10. When should I come?
11. At first their dishes did not suit my taste.
12. What he says does not worry me at all.

LESSON V

1. He got up at 7:30 and went to the office at 8 as usual.
2. If you feel ill, you had better go home and lie down.
3. I took medicine in the morning and my fever went down in the afternoon.
4. Thinking that he would need it, I brought it here for him.
5. May I have a look at it?
6. We sometimes feel dizzy, if we are hungry.
7. No wonder I had a chill.
8. I ran a high fever because my throat was swollen.
9. He could not come because of the heavy snow.
10. Take this medicine between meals.
11. This shot will bring your fever down, I assure you.
12. It is not very expensive, but of poor quality.
13. We talked about what we had read in the newspapers.

14. You must pay more attention to what you eta.
15. He plays golf over the weekend, wet or fine.
16. Everybody was relieved at the news.
17. I advise you to take it easy for a couple of days, even if you have no fever.

LESSON VI

1. There is one thing I would like to ask you about.
2. When should I go to buy it?
3. She was kind enough to show me how to use it.
4. It does not make any difference whether he comes or not.
5. I did read it, but I do not remember it now.
6. Chopsticks may perhaps be easier to eat with.
7. I have just eaten supper and am not hungry.
8. The man who is standing in front of the store has just come from Toronto.
9. Let me know how things are going with you.
10. His questions often beat me.
11. I wish I could speak Japanese as well as you do.
12. He came here on business and has been staying at this hotel.
13. It is I, and not you, who should help him.
14. I think I will stay home and write letters because the weather is bad.
15. I think I will eat it later.
16. Most of my friends have made plans for the winter vacation.
17. I hope it will turn out as everybody wishes.
18. He seems to be able to speak English well.
19. Let's take off before it gets dark.
20. She was so deep in conversation with me that she forgot to give you a ring.
21. If you go straight ahead and take the second turning to the right, you will see a pink building on your left.
22. Even if you read the sentence twice, you may perhaps not understand the meaning of it.
23. Transfer at the next station to the Tōkaidō Line, if you want to take an express.
24. I'll have something, say, deep-fried prawns for lunch.

25. Speaking of trains, the fastest train in Japan travels at a speed of 130 miles an hour.
26. I understand he has to go to the hospital every other day.
27. I could talk to him on the telephone; so I don't have to write him a letter.
28. All the students are supposed to know it.
29. These buses seldom run on schedule.
30. As you know, words of foreign origin such as 'koppu' and 'pan' are written in "katakana".
31. As a rule, I do not take sugar in my coffee.
32. The price varies according to size.
33. If one does not know the customs of a country in which one resides, one will sometimes be confused.
34. This is entirely different from the one I have.

LESSON VII

1. Do you have anything on tomorrow evening?
2. I have nothing special to say.
3. We had fine weather after a long rain.
4. I wish I could do so.
5. I was treated to 'sukiyaki' at his home last week.
6. There were nothing but small ones. I needed big ones.
7. He woke up late and came without eating breakfast.
8. She went shopping without saying what time she would come home.
9. You had better not bother him because he is busy.
10. Don't throw it away; you took so much trouble to make it.
11. Please do not force him to walk.
12. If you go this early, you will inconvenience him.

LESSON VIII

1. Would you like to get there by 3?
2. The next chapter seems long and difficult.
3. It looks like snow.
4. I have a cold, but it is nothing serious.
5. He is thinking of becoming a lawyer.

6. He writes to the effect that he will come to Canada this summer.
7. I am under the impression that the man who wrote this novel is Japanese.
8. He had no appetite because of a high fever.
9. What do you think about the short skirts which are in fashion now?
10. Some of the pictures you took a few months ago are in today's papers.

LESSON IX

1. It has been raining on and off these two days.
2. I sometimes watch TV and sometimes read magazines.
3. All of these three houses are too expensive, I'm afraid.
4. There are occasions on which I drink beer after taking a bath.
5. There were both warm days and cold days.
6. Some people rested, and others worked.
7. It being Sunday, all the stores are closed except drug stores.
8. If it is not fine weather, I do not want to go.
9. He is in the habit of taking a walk before breakfast, if it is not rainy.
10 You should be careful not to drink too much.
11. I prepared my lessons after doing the dishes.
12. He says he will help me move into the new house.
13. Tōkyō is the largest of all the cities in Japan.
14. The smaller it is, the more expensive it is.
15. The more you speak it, the more fluent you will become in it.
16. The colder it becomes, the redder these leaves become.

LESSON X

1. It is a little too hot for this time of the year, isn't it?
2. We had to change our plan because it started raining.
3. I have just arrived at the station.
4. I have met you before, but can't quite place you.
5. Please try to come by 5 tomorrow afternoon.
6. Nobody came while you were away.

7. She speaks Japanese with a German accent.
8. Repetition is most essential to the study of foreign languages.
9. She said nothing about you.
10. We were made to read it five times.
11. Pay more attention to what I say.
12. It is natural that he should get mad.
13. It was difficult for me to translate these complicated Japanese sentences into English.
14. I make it a rule not to go out on Saturday mornings.

LESSON XI

1. This city had a small population before World War II.
2. My room faces south and is pretty warm on fine days.
3. Many independent nations were born on the African Continent after World War II.
4. Buddhism, which was introduced into Japan in 552, exerted a great influence on the Japanese way of thinking.
5. This province is twice as large as my country.
6. A long time ago China ranked in civilization with Egypt.
7. He seems to know you well.
8. English is not spoken in some countries in South America.
9. Nearly every Japanese college student can read English fairly well, but cannot speak it well.
10. We may safely say that "hiragana" are easier to read than "katakana".

LESSON XII

1. We talked over coffee for several hours.
2. Can you read Japanese newspapers without consulting a dictionary?
3. That means, in short, that he is not going with us, doesn't it?
4. The new hotel was named Ōtani in honour of Mr. Ōtani, the president.
5. What I noticed in Tōkyō was that there were a large number of cabs.
6. You had better wash it because it is covered with dust.

7. Let's have a crack at it anyway, shall we?
8. Such things as gloves, neckties, and socks are on display at the store.
9. You do not realize why this is expensive unless you compare this with yours.
10. Somebody is at the door. Go and see who it is.
11. These Japanese sentences were so complicated that it took me two hours to translate them into English.
12. You should be careful not to leave a bad impression on him.
13. Don't you think what he is saying now is wrong?
14. For several reasons he does not want to sign the paper.
15. She has to read not only "hiragana" but also "kanji".
16. They not only sell cars but buy them.
17. The house which he is about to buy is not only small but old.
18. She can not only speak it, but can write it.
19. I not only heard it; I saw it, too.
20. The heavy snow prevented me from attending the conference.
21. According to a friend of mine who is in Kyōto, it is still cold there.
22. They say this is the best hospital in this country.
23. It seldom rains in Tōkyō in winter.
24. I wonder if he is not sick.
25. We wonder if she does not know it.
26. I do not know when and where.
27. He said he would be here by 5 without fail.
28. They did not tell me why they did not come.
29. She made many purchases and has no money left.
30. There were no stores to speak of in this town when I was a child.
31. According to the weather forecast, this fine weather won't last long.

LESSON XIII

1. When I got to his office, he was about to leave.
2. He married a cousin of mine last year and lives in the suburbs of Tōkyō.
3. Is there anything you want?

4. Thinking that he might know it, I asked him.
5. Some "hiragana" are awfully hard to write.
6. I wondered what I should do, in case he did not show up.
7. From the viewpoint of the Japanese, the custom may perhaps be rather queer.
8. The child looked very happy when he got his birthday present from his parents.
9. He seems to have made up his mind to travel with me.
10. When it comes to "kanji", I am lost.
11. Let me know whether it is convenient for you or not.
12. I'm sure they will fix my broken umbrella while I wait.
13. He talks as if he knew everything, doesn't he?
14. This necktie is too loud for me. Could you trade it for a quiet one?
15. After all, she is my sister and I think I have to help her.
16. There was nothing but stale bread in the store.
17. Are those Japanese students who desire to study abroad increasing in number?

LESSON XIV

1. The capital of a country is the main city where the government is.
2. It is said that their manners and customs are entirely different from ours.
3. One should not enter a Japanese-style house with one's shoes on.
4. If you always exaggerate, people won't believe what you say.
5. All of my friends who went there on a trip were surprised at it being cold.
6. The patient is getting worse and worse.
7. I want you to make this shorter.
8. The mayor is wondering how he can beautify the city.
9. Shall I make your tea a little stronger?
10. Canada is the richest country in the world after the U.S.A.

LESSON XV

1. Wondering what time it was, he took a look at his watch.
2. No matter how difficult the job may be, he intends to finish it in two weeks or so.
3. However hard he works, he does not get tired.
4. No matter how gorgeous the hotel is, I don't want to stay there for more than a week.
5. Do it by all means before you go to bed tonight.
6. When I gave him a piece of advice, he looked mad.
7. I saw you mail a letter.
8. Watch me do it, please.
9. Have you ever heard her sing?
10. I am much obliged to him.
11. If he had had money, he would have bought a better car.
12. If it had been fine weather yesterday, we would have played golf.
13. It is not a place worth visiting.
14. I am positive that he knows it.
15. The book is so thick that I cannot finish reading it in a day.
16. I have a strong desire to make a tour of the world.
17. If the heat is unbearable, you had better not stay too long.
18. My father told me to show the guest around the campus.
19. Put your raincoat on so that you won't get wet.
20. She cannot be that young.
21. I almost forgot my appointment.
22. What you said weighed on my mind so heavily that I could hardly sleep last night.
23. Please go and see if he is there.
24. My uncle wanted to become a newspaper reporter when young.

LESSON XVI

1. Just as you drink coffee, we Japanese drink green tea.
2. Customs vary with countries.
3. There are some people who do not eat meat on Fridays.
4. Our rice may perhaps be equivalent to bread in the West.

5. I am thinking of going shopping on the Ginza after writing a letter to Mr. Koyama.

6. No rules are free from exceptions.

7. Some Westerners wrote books on Japan in the Meiji period— Chamberlain and Hearn, for example.

8. She says she does not know me, despite the fact that she has seen me many times.

9. Traffic accidents in large cities are increasing in number year by year.

10. He looked as if nothing had happened.

11. I am afraid it will begin snowing before I get home.

12. I cannot find any words to thank you for coming all the way to see me off.

13. Custom requires a man to rise from his seat when a woman enters a room.

14. Nothing is more disagreeable than flies and mosquitos.

15. Try to be back home as early as possible.

16. Maybe he felt inclined to get some rest after working hard.

17. The police believe that the driver's carelessness caused the car accident.

18. We had no choice but to do as we were told.

19. If you had not lent me a helping hand, I could not have finished it yesterday.

20. San Francisco, located in the western part of the U.S., is considered to be the most beautiful city in North America.

21. We borrowed six cups from you, but we are still two cups short.

22. He speaks Spanish, not to mention English and French.

23. Pearl Buck has won world-wide fame as a novelist.

24. He says in his letter that he is looking forward to seeing me in Tōkyō next month.

LESSON XVII

1. Upon graduation from Keiō University in 1965, he was employed by the Pacific Trading Co. Ltd.

2. It is three years since his daughter was killed in a traffic accident.

3. The American economist is planning on doing research on Japan's economic policies in pre-World War II days.
4. He, who majored in political science, is writing a thesis on the diplomatic history of the Orient.
5. No matter how hard you may study Japanese, you won't be able to read Japanese papers in a year.
6. However cold it may be, you had better not sleep with all the windows closed.
7. Thinking that it might be suitable, I bought it.
8. Thinking that it might rain, I brought an umbrella with me.
9. We tried to take a good look at it, but there was such a crowd that we could not do so.
10. People are beginning to forget how dreadful a war is.
11. Perhaps (It may happen that) I shall not return tonight.
12. I have been to the post office to mail a letter.
13. I missed the 9:25 train by a few minutes.
14. I do not doubt that what he says is true.
15. I can't help thinking that he is still alive.
16. He has neither seen nor heard it.
17. I can neither speak nor write German.
18. This beef-steak is neither tough nor tender.
19. He is neither rich nor poor.
20. I am sure it will be in the papers tomorrow.
21. There is no particular reason why these children have grown taller.
22. It looked like rain this morning; so I dropped the idea of going on a hike.
23. I want you to help me when I am in trouble.
24. Higher prices have resulted from the new economic policy of the government.
25. Apart from "kanji", what bothers you in your study of Japanese?
26. He seldom keeps promises; therefore nobody seems to trust him.
27. We cannot very well reduce the price because there is a great demand for it.

LESSON XVIII

1. He never fails to give me a buzz when he comes up to Tōkyō.
2. It is not very hot, but fairly humid.
3. We are apt to forget that we have to pay attention to what we eat and drink.
4. We have more precipitation in September than in the rainy season. The reason for this is that typhoons hit Japan in the early fall.
5. Thanks to your advice, I got well much sooner than my doctor had thought.
6. The word "kara-tsuyu" means a rainy season without any rainfall.
7. There were cases in which I had to consult this dictionary.

LESSON XIX

1. The food at the country inn where I stayed was beyond words unpalatable.
2. Do you mean to say that I do not have to do it?
3. Every time I see this picture, I think of my home town.
4. As the number of cars increases, traffic becomes heavier.
5. With the progress of civilization, our life becomes more complicated.
6. I was in no mood to eat supper perhaps because I had a headache.
7. He lost confidence in his own ability and killed himself.
8. If only he had been careful, the accident would not have occurred.
9. If only you read it, you would understand it.
10. When you are in Hokkaidō, you will feel as if you were in Canada.

LESSON XX

1. There was a large attendance at the concert in spite of the downpour.

2. The isolation policy of the Shōgunate proved to be a serious hindrance to the progress of Japan's learning and civilization.
3. He made it a principle to use as simple words as possible in writing his books.
4. As a result of his many years' researches, he invented the machine.
5. It goes without saying that he made greater endeavour than anybody else towards promoting friendly relations between Britain and Japan.
6. It would be no exaggeration to say that Japan underwent a complete change during the Meiji period.
7. He will remain in our memory as a man who rendered great services to our country.

LESSON XXI

1. My apologies for not writing to you earlier.
2. I have nothing in particular to do this evening; so please stay as long as you can.
3. He is apparently tired after a long trip.
4. He parents expect too much of me.
5. You can take home anything you find in this room.
6. Drop me a line telling me how things have been with you.

LESSON XXII

1. Far from reading the letter which I took so much trouble to write, he did not even look at it.
2. It is quite reasonable that an adult has to place emphasis upon grammar in his attempt to learn a foreign language.
3. "Kuchi ga jōzu da." is one of the Japanese idioms which if translated word for word into English make no sense to English-speaking people.
4. I am sure he will get to the point where he will have no difficulty in expressing himself in Japanese.
5. If you do not practice speaking the language you are learning for fear of making mistakes, you won't be able to acquire fluency in it.

6. You should have expressed your opinion.

7. I do not remember having said so.

8. She became a good speaker of Japanese by taking advantage of every opportunity to speak it.

LESSON XXIII

1. The international organization which was established after World War II is aimed at introducing Japanese culture to Western countries.

2. The United Nations was established for the purpose of promoting world peace and cultural interchange among the nations of the world.

3. Japan's representative novels have been translated into English so that even those who have no knowledge of Japanese can appreciate them.

4. I have read some of the Japanese classics in translation.

5. There is a strong possibility that an agreement will be concluded between Waseda University and this university on the exchange of students.

6. The two governments seem to have reached an agreement on the peaceful uses of atomic energy.

7. Lafcadio Hearn was one of the greatest interpreters of Japan for the Western world.

LESSON XXIV

1. It does not rain heavily during the rainy season which lasts for a month.

2. She said she nearly forgot her appointment to see me this afternoon.

3. There is no fear that the typhoon will hit the southern districts of Japan.

4. There were cases where travellers were robbed of their money while travelling.

5. Travelling by train is more comfortable and less expensive than travelling by bus in Japan, where roads are not as good as those on the North American Continent.

LESSON XXV

1. The Japanese Diet consists of elected members who represent the whole nation.
2. Our constitution stipulates that a general election should take place within forty days after the Diet is dissolved.
3. This should not be used except in an emergency.
4. Reserve funds are disbursed only when something unforeseen has occurred.
5. The bill of non-confidence in the cabinet was okayed by the Lower House and the cabinet decided to resign in a body.
6. I will leave for Tōkyō tomorrow afternoon unless I get sick.

LESSON XXVI

1. This province is known throughout the world as an apple-producing area.
2. We were deeply impressed by his ability to write poems.
3. Nobody could match him in the knowledge of English grammar.
4. The Buddhist priest has a high reputation for learning.
5. May I suggest that you marry the man who loves you so much?
6. At the suggestion of Dr. A, he wrote about what he had observed during his two-month trip through the Far East.
7. I took a great interest in their quaint manners and customs.
8. Canada is, to a certain extent, Americanized in the eyes of the British people.
9. Needless to say, I expressed my thanks to him for his assistance.
10. There is perhaps no denying the fact that he looked into our legends before writing his book.

LESSON XXVII

1. Mr. Gold, who is one of the millionaires now, was nothing but a poor peasant 50 years ago.

2. Along with the betterment of women's social position in Japan in post-war days, there has been a tremendous increase in the number of girls receiving higher education.
3. Some people are of the opinion that the new educational system does not fit in with Japan.
4. You will fail in the examinations unless you work hard. :
5. It is a common practice for us to serve our guests with tea and cake, when they drop in.

LESSON XXVIII

1. Do not worry about what he says.
2. I bumped into your brother on my way home from school and was surprised to hear that you had been hurt in a traffic accident.
3. I'm afraid I will have to be operated on, if I continue to have fever.
4. How can you talk to me like that?
5. You have my sympathy.
6. My doctor says that I will be discharged from the hospital in a week or two.

LESSON XXIX

1. Typhoons which originate in the South Pacific areas often hit Japan in autumn, inflicting heavy damage on her rice crop.
2. One will be surprised to know that Japan, in spite of her being a small country, produces the richest variety of fruits next to the U.S.A.
3. Japan is so poor in mineral resources that she has to import a large quantity of coal, iron, copper, etc. from other countries, Canada and Australia in particular.
4. The greatest drawback to the development of her industries is that she lacks basic materials such as iron and oil.
5. The government will have to take steps to cope with the shortage of meat and dairy products which has been produced by changes in the citizens' eating habits in post-war days.

6. Most countries cannot maintain their existence unless they have close economic relations with other countries.
7. I have to admit that Japan had a bad reputation for her shoddy products in pre-war days.

LESSON XXX

1. During the Nara period, Buddhist priests in Nara became so involved in state politics that the government was forced to move the capital from Nara to Kyōto.
2. In the famous Hōryūji Temple, the oldest wooden structure in the world, we find Indian, Chinese, Persian, and Greek styles of architecture.
3. When the relations between Japan and China ceased to exist, the Chinese civilization which had been introduced into Japan came to take on Japanese character.
4. Zen Buddhism, in which the keynote is self-understanding and self-reliance, gained popularity among the 'samurai' in the Kamakura period.
5. Japan's first contact with the West occurred on a small island south of Kagoshima, where several Portugese landed after their ship was severely damaged by a typhoon.
6. Ieyasu Tokugawa, founder of the Edo Shōgunate, placed a ban on Christianity for fear that it would destroy feudalism which he had taken pains to establish.
7. Some of those who pursued the study of "Western learning" were critical of the Shōgunate's policies.
8. A period was put to Japan's 200-year-long isolation policy when the Shōgunate government concluded a treaty with the US government in 1854.
9. The conservatives maintain that the Constitution should be revised on the ground that it was forced upon Japan after her defeat in World War II.
10. Japan has been extending financial and technical assistance to several less developed countries in Asia in the hope of contributing to world peace and human happiness.

CONJUGATION TABLES

Group I ("*Godan*") Verbs

Endings	Examples	Stems	Base 1	Base 2	Base 3	Base 4	Base 5	Base 6	Base 7	Base 8
bu	yobu (call)	yo-	ba	bi	bu	be	bō	nde	nda	be
gu	oyogu (swim)	oyo-	ga	gi	gu	ge	gō	ide	ida	ge
ku	kaku (write)	ka-	ka	ki	ku	ke	kō	ite	ita	ke
mu	nomu (drink)	no-	ma	mi	mu	me	mō	nde	nda	me
nu	shinu (die)	shi-	na	ni	nu	ne	nō	nde	nda	ne
ru	uru (sell)	u-	ra	ri	ru	re	rō	tte	tta	re
su	hanasu (speak)	hana-	sa	shi	su	se	sō	shite	shita	se
tsu	motsu (hold)	mo-	ta	chi	tsu	te	tō	tte	tta	te
u	kau (buy)	ka-	wa	i	u	e	ō	tte	tta	e
eru	kaeru (return)	kae-	ra	ri	ru	re	rō	tte	tta	re
iru	hairu (enter)	hai-	ra	ri	ru	re	rō	tte	tta	re

Group II ("*Ichidan*") Verbs

Endings	Examples	Stems	Base 1	Base 2	Base 3	Base 4	Base 5	Base 6	Base 7	Base 8
eru	taberu (eat)	tab-	e	e	eru	ere	eyō	ete	eta	ero
iru	miru (see)	m-	i	i	iru	ire	iyō	ite	ita	iro

Irregular Verbs

Examples	Stems	Base 1	Base 2	Base 3	Base 4	Base 5	Base 6	Base 7	Base 8
kuru (come)	k-	o	i	uru	ure	oyō	ite	ita	oi
suru (do)	s-	hi	hi	uru	ure	hiyō	hite	hita	hiro

Base 1 – Negative
Base 2 – Connective, Noun-forming
Base 3 – Dictionary form (Verb-root)
Base 4 – Conditional
Base 5 – Volitional, Conjectural
Base 6 – "*Te*"-form
Base 7 – "*Ta*"-form, Frequentative
Base 8 – Imperative

CONJUGATION TABLES

True Adjectives

Examples	Stems	Base 1	Base 2	Base 3	Base 4	Base 5	Base 6	Base 7
akai (red)	aka-	ku	ku	i	kere	karō	kute	katta
ōkii (big)	ōki-	ku	ku	i	kere	karō	kute	katta

Base 1 - Negative
Base 2 - Adverbial
Base 3 - Dictionary form
Base 4 - Conditional

Base 5 - Conjectural
Base 6 - "Te"-form
Base 7 - "Ta"-form, Frequentative

Quasi-Adjectives

Examples	Stems	Base 1	Base 2	Base 3	Base 4	Base 5	Base 6	Base 7	Base 8
shizuka-na (quiet)	shizuka	de (ja)	ni	na	da	nara	darō	de	datta
futsū-no (ordinary)	futsū	de (ja)	ni	no	da	nara	darō	de	datta

Base 1 - Negative
Base 2 - Adverbial
Base 3 - Dictionary form
Base 4 - Conclusive

Base 5 - Conditional
Base 6 - Conjectural
Base 7 - "Te"-form
Base 8 - "Ta"-form, Frequentative

FUNCTIONAL GRAMMAR

bakari

1. (approximately)

Ninen bakari imashita.   I was there for two years or so.

2. (only; nothing but)

Kodomo bakari kimashita.   Only children came.

Asonde bakari imasu.   He does nothing but enjoying himself.

3. *bakari da* (did something just now) ← after the plain past form of a verb

Tabeta bakari desu.   I have just eaten it.

4. *bakari de nakute* (or *naku*) .... *mo* (not only .... but) ← a noun precedes *bakari* and *mo*

Eigo bakari de naku, Furansu-go mo dekimasu.   He speaks not only English, but French.

5. *bakari de nakute* (or *naku*) (not only .... but) ← after verbs or true adjectives

Yomu bakari de nakute, kaki-masu.   He not only reads it but writes it.

Takai bakari de naku, warui n desu.   It is not only expensive but is of poor quality.

6. *de aru bakari de nakute* (or *naku*) (not only .... but) ← after a noun or the stem of a quasi-adjective

Seijika de aru bakari de naku, gakusha deshita.   He was not only a statesman but a scholar.

Kono ryokan wa shizuka de   This inn is not only quiet, but

aru bakari de nakute, kirei   is clean.
desu.

The word *bakari* in 4., 5., and 6. can be replaced by *dake.*

de

1. (in; at) — place
Tōkyō de mita n desu ka?   Did you see it in Tokyo?

2. (in — time required)
Ichijikan de ikeru deshō.   You will be able to get there
                               in an hour.

3. (at; for — figures)
Nihyaku-en de kaimashita.   I bought it for 200 yen.
Mittsu de shinda n desu.   He died at three years old.

4. (by; with — means)
Chikatetsu de ikimashō ka?   Shall we go by subway?
Nihongo de kaite mo ii desu   May I write in Japanese?
ka?

5. (out of; of — material)
'Sake' wa nan de tsukuru n   What is 'sake' made from?
desu ka?

6. (through — reason or cause)
Byōki de ikenakatta n desu.   I could not go because of sick-
                               ness.

7. (by — measure)
Kono rōdōshatachi wa jikan   Do these laborers work by the
de hataraku n desu ka?   hour?

8. (condition or state)

Kore de ii n desu ka?   Is this O.K.?

9. (and; but) ← for connecting clauses

A-san wa Amerikajin de, B-   Mr. A is American and Mr. B
san wa Supeinjin desu.   is Spanish.
Asa wa ame de, hiru kara   It will be rainy in the morn-
hare desu.   ing, but will be fine in the
     afternoon.

10. (among)

Nihon no depāto de gaikoku   There are some Japanese de-
ni shiten o dashite iru no ga   partment stores which have
arimasu.   established branches abroad.

demo, de mo

1. (even)

Kodomo demo shitte iru deshō.   Perhaps even a child knows
     it.

2. (or something, somebody, etc.)

Ocha demo nomimashō.   Let's drink tea or something.

3. (however) ← at the beginning of a sentence

Demo chotto tōi desu.   It is a little far, though.

4. (even if) ← after a noun or the stem of a quasi-adjective

Ame demo ikimasu.   Even if it is rainy weather, I
     will go.

Jōzu demo mainichi renshū   Even if you are good at it,
shinasai.   practise it every day.

5. *de mo .... de mo* (whether .... or; either .... or) ← after
a noun or the stem of quasi-adjectives

Doyō de mo nichiyō de mo   Either Saturday or Sunday
kekkō desu.   will do.

6. *de mo* ... *de mo* (neither .... nor) ← the final *de mo* is
followed by negative

Nihonjin de mo chūgokujin de I hear he is neither Japanese
mo nai sō desu.   nor Chinese.

ga

1. (after the subject)

Kore ga ii deshō.   This will be good.

2. (but; and) ← for connecting clauses

Kurai deshita ga, miemashita. It was dark, but I could see.
Ryōhō arimasu ga, dotchi ga I have both, and which do you
osuki desu ka?   prefer?

3. (used at the end of a sentence to know the other party's
reaction to the speaker's remark)

Inta arimasen ga.   We do not have it now (and
what shall I do, or what do
you wish to have me do?).

4. (at the end of a subjunctive sentence)

Okane ga areba, ikimasu ga. If I had money, I would go.
Okane ga areba, itta n desu If I had had money, I would
ga.   have gone.

5. (after the subject in a subordinate clause)

Ame ga furu to, michi wa If it rains, the road becomes
doro-darake ni narimasu. muddy.

6. (after interrogative pronouns such as *nani* (what?),
donata (or *dare*) (who?), *dotchi* (or *dochira*) (which one

of the two?), *dore* (which one of the three or more?), *dono* (which one?), *donna* (what kind?), *doko* (where?), *itsu* (when?), etc., when they are used in the nominative case)

Nani ga haitte imasu ka?	What is in it?
Donata ga ikimasu ka?	Who will go?
Dore ga ichiban yasui n desu ka?	Which is the cheapest?

7. (before words such as *aru* (own), *dekiru* (possible), *iru* (need), *wakaru* (understand), *hoshii* (desirous), *kowai* (fearful), *kirai* (dislike), *suki* (like), etc., except in the case of contrast)

Kuruma ga aru n desu ka?	Does he have a car?
Eigo ga yoku dekimasu.	He is fluent in English.
Kasa ga iru deshō.	You will need an umbrella.
Nihongo ga wakarimasu ne.	He understands Japanese, doesn't he?
Mizu ga hoshii n desu.	I want a glass of water.
Kodomo wa inu ga kowai yō desu.	The child seems to be afraid of the dog.
Aburakkoi mono ga kirai da sō desu.	I understand he is not fond of greasy foods.
Ōkii no ga suki kamo shiremasen.	He may like the big one.

8. (used in the potential construction except in the case of contrast)

Doitsugo ga hanasemasu ka?	Can you speak German?

There is a new trend among the young generation toward the use of *o* in place of *ga* in the above construction, which may be frowned upon by some sticklers for grammar.

Compare (a) with (b):

(a)	*Eigo ga dekimasu.*	He speaks English.

ぁ) *Eigo wa dekimasu.*   He speaks English (but not French, etc.).

gurai

1. (about; approximately)

Nijikan gurai kakaru deshō.   It will take about two hours.
Kono hō ga ii gurai desu.   I'd think this is better.

2. (as ... as)

Kore gurai ōkii desu ka?   Is it as large as this?

3. (extent; so ... that)

Taberarenai gurai attan desu.   There was so much that we could not eat.

hodo

1. (approximately)

Gofun hodo kakarimashita.   It took about five minutes.

2. (as .... as)

Koko wa otaku hodo shizuka ja arimasen.   This place is not as quiet as your home.

Broadly speaking, *hodo* is used in the negative, whereas *gurai* in the affirmative.

3. (extent)

Arukenai hodo konde imashita.   It was crowded to the extent that I could hardly walk.
Tōkyō hodo nigiyaka-na tokoro wa nai deshō.   There will be no place so bustling as Tokyo.

4. (the ... the ...)

Yasukerebera, yasui hodo ii.   The cheaper, the better.
Nomeba, nomu hodo yoku   The more she drinks, the more
shaberimasu.   she chatters.

Sometimes the first conditional clause is left out.

iku

1. (go)

Itsu ikimashita ka?   When did you go?

2. *ni iku* (go to do something) ← after the 2nd base of a verb
   or a noun

Mi ni ikitai desu ka?   Would you like to go to see it?
Ginza e kaimono ni ikimashita.   She went shopping on the
                                   Ginza.

3. *-te iku* (keep on)

Kuruma wa fuete iku deshō.   The number of cars will keep
                                   on growing.

ka

1. (denotes interrogation)

Ii desu ka?   Is it good?

2. (or)

Kyō ka ashita kite kudasai.   Please come today or tomor-
                                   row.

3. (indicates uncertainty)
Yuki ga furu ka to omoima-   I thought it might snow.
shita.

4. *ka .... ka* (whether .... or)

Takai ka takakunai ka shiri-masen.   I do not know whether it is expensive or not.

Ii gakkō ka dō ka oshiete kudasai.   Please tell me whether it is a good school or not.

Yomeru ka dō ka kikimashō ka?   Shall I ask him whether he can read it or not?

kara

1. (from)

Anata no ojisan kara morai-mashita.   I got it from your uncle.

2. (since; from) — time

Kugatsu kara imasu.   I have been here since September.

3. (because) ← after a verb or an adjective

Omoi kara, motemasen.   I cannot carry it because it is heavy.

Ame ga futta kara, samuku natta n desu.   It became cold because it rained.

4. *da kara* (because) ← after a noun or the stem of a quasi-adjective

Ii tenki da kara, sanpo ni dekakemashō.   Let's go out for a walk because it is fine weather.

Binbō da kara, kaenai n desu.   I cannot buy it, because I am poor.

5. *-te kara* (after -ing)

Ohiru o tabete kara ikimasu.   I will go after eating lunch.

Koko e kite kara ichinen ni narimasu.   It is one year since I came here.

Caution must be exercised not to confuse (a) with (b)

in the following:

(a) *tabeta kara*   because one ate
(b) *tabete kara*   after one eats

koto

1. (matter; thing; fact)

Anata no itta koto wa wasure-   I will not forget what you
masen.   said.

    Koto generally refers to abstract things, whereas *mono* denotes concrete and material things.

2. *koto ga* (or *mo*) *aru* (sometimes) ← after the dictionary form of verbs or adjectives

Hayaku neru koto ga arimasu.   I sometimes go to bed early.
Samui koto mo arimasu.   It sometimes is cold.
Kion ga ijō-na koto ga ari-   The temperature was some-
mashita.   times abnormal.

3. *koto ga* (or *mo*) *ōi* (often) ← after the dictionary form of verbs or adjectives

Sō iu fū ni kangaeru koto ga   We often think that way.
ōi n desu.
Ima goro konna-ni atsui koto   It is seldom this hot about this
wa sukunai n desu.   time of the year.

4. *koto ga aru* (have done something) ← after the plain past form of a verb

Mita koto ga arimasu ka?   Have you ever seen it?
Itta koto ga arimasen.   I have never been there.

5. *koto ni naru* (be decided; be arranged) ← after the dictionary form of a verb

Nara e hikkosu koto ni nari-   It has become necessary for
mashita.   me to move to Nara.

6. *koto ni suru* (decide) ← after the dictionary form of a verb

Kau koto ni shimashita.   I have decided to buy it.

7. *koto ni suru* (assume) ← after the plain past form of a verb

Koko ni ita koto ni shimashō.   Let's assume that you were here.

8. *koto ni shite iru* (make it a rule to . . . .) ← after the dictionary form of a verb

Maiasa kudamono o taberu koto ni shite imasu.   I make it a rule to eat fruit every morning.

9. *to iu koto da* (they say; I hear) ← after verbs or true adjectives

Raishū kuru to iu koto desu.   I hear he is coming next week.
Muzukashii to iu koto desu.   I understand it is difficult.

10. *da to iu koto da* (they say; I hear) ← after a noun or the stem of a quasi-adjective

Mezurashi namae da to iu koto desu.   They say it is an uncommon name.
Goshujin wa byōki da to iu koto desu.   Her husband is sick, I understand.

11. (emphatic)

Takai koto wa takai desu ga, ii n desu.   It is expensive as far as that goes, but is good.
Kita koto wa kita n desu ga, sugu dekakemashita.   He did come, but went out right away.
Yakamashii koto wa arimasen.   It is *not* noisy.

12. (exclamatory)

Atsui koto.   How hot!

Taberu koto.   How he eats!

kuru

1. (come)

Itsu kuru ka shirimasen.   I do not know when he will
                                come.

2. *ni kuru* (come to do something) ← after the 2nd base of
   a verb or a noun

Hana o kai ni kita n desu.   I came to buy flowers.
Sanpo ni kimashita.   He came here for a walk.

3. *-te kuru* (come towards; go and do something — motion
   towards the speaker)

Mite kite kudasai.   Go and see, please.
Kado no mise de katte kima-   I went to the store on the
   shita.   corner and bought it.

4. *-te kuru* (become; come to; grow)

Onaka ga suite kimashita.   I became hungry. (or I am
                                hungry.)
Gogo ame ga futte kuru deshō. It will begin raining in the
                                afternoon.

The expression *-te kuru* refers to 'coming into existence',
the idea of coming being vague.

5. *to kitara* (when it comes to) ← after a noun

Eigo to kitara, marukkiri da- When it comes to English, I
me desu.   do not know a single word.

miru

1. (look; see)

Nani o mite imasu ka?   What are you looking at?

2. *te miru* (do and see; try to)

Tabete mimashō.   Let's eat it and see how it
                                    tastes.

Akete mimasu.   (a) I will open it and see
                                        what is in it.

                                   (b) I will try to open it.

The context determines whether (a) or (b) is meant.

mo

1. (too; also)

Ano hito mo tomodachi desu.   He is also a friend of mine.

2. (not .... either) ← followed by negative

Kore mo suki ja nai n desu.   I do not like this either.

3. (even) ← after a noun

Shinbun mo yoku yomemasu.   He can read even a newspaper
                               well.

4. *mo suru* (do even) ← after the 2nd base of a verb

Kanji o kaki mo shimasu.   He even writes 'kanji'.
Mi mo shinakatta n desu.   She did not even look at it.

5. (as much, many, etc. as)

Hyakunin mo kimashita.   As many as one hundred
                              people came.

6. (about; or so)

Gofun mo sureba, kaeru de-   He will come back in five min-
shō.   utes or so.

7. *mo .... mo* (both .... and) ← after nouns

A-san mo B-san mo kimashita.   Both Mr. A and Mr. B came.

8. *mo* .... *mo* (neither .... nor) ← after nouns. Negative should follow the final *mo*.

Eigo mo Furansugo mo hana-   He can speak neither Eng-
semasen.   lish nor French.

9. *mo* .... *mo* (both .... and) ← after the adverbial form of adjectives

Hayaku mo osoku mo ugoki-   It moves both fast and slow-
masu.   ly.
Hade-ni mo jimi-ni mo nari-   It becomes both bright and
masu.   quiet.

10. *mo* .... *mo* (neither .... nor) ← after the adverbial form of adjectives. Negative should follow the final *mo*.

Tōku mo chikaku mo nai n   It is neither far nor near.
desu.

11. *mo* .... *mo suru* (do both .... and) ← after the 2nd base of verbs

Yomi mo kaki mo shimasu.   He reads it and writes it as
     well.

12. *mo* .... *mo shinai* (do neither .... nor) ← after the 2nd base of verbs

Akanbō wa naki mo warai mo   The baby neither cries nor
shimasen.   smiles.

13. *de mo* .... *de mo.* See *de mo*

14. *te mo.* See *te*-form

15. *te mo* .... *te mo ii* (may either .... or)

Saki-ni itte mo matte mo ii   You may either go ahead or
desu.   wait.

16. *te mo* .... *te mo ikenai* (must neither .... nor)

Aruite mo hashitte mo ikema- You must neither walk nor
sen. run.

See the following patterns:

Utte mo katte mo imasu. They are selling and buying
as well.

Aratte mo hoshite mo arima- It is neither washed nor dried.
sen.

17. *te mo* .... *te mo* (whether .... or)

Futte mo tette mo, kimasu. I will come, rain or shine.
Yokute mo warukute mo, ka- I have to buy it, whether it
wanakereba naranai n desu. is good or bad.

18. *te mo* .... *te mo* (no matter how)

Yatte mo yatte mo, dame No matter how hard I may
desu. try, I won't succeed.

Note the repetition of the same verb.

19. *ikura* (or *donna-ni*) .... *te mo* (no matter how)

Ikura matasarete mo, okori- No matter how long he is kept
masen. waiting, he does not get
mad.

20. The idea of *mo* in the affirmative is sometimes indistinct
and weaker than *wa*:

Gakkō mo raishū natsuyasu- Your school will break up for
mi desu ne. the summer holidays next
week, I presume.

mono

1. (thing; goods)

Mezurashii mono o mitsuke- You found a rare article,
mashita ne. didn't you?

2. (fellow; person)

Yamada to iu mono   a man called Yamada

3. (sometimes used in the abstract sense)

Mono o shiranai no ni wa odo-   I was surprised at his igno-
rokimashita.   rance of the ways of the
     world.

4. *mono da* is used to add emphasis to the desiderative form.

Issho-ni ikitai mono desu ne.   I wish I could go with you. (I
     would like to go with you.)

Mono is often shortened to *mon* in familiar speech.

5. *mono da* (used to ...) ← after the plain past form of a
verb

Kodomo no toki ni yoku kita   I used to come here when a
mono desu.   child.

6. *mono da* (ought to ...) ← after the dictionary form of
a verb

Kodomo wa oya no iu koto o   A child should obey his par-
kiku mono desu yo.   ents, you understand?

7. *mono ja nai* (must not) ← after the dictionary form of a
verb

Sonna zasshi o yomu mono ja   You should not read such a
arimasen.   magazine.

8. *mono desu ka* (or *mono ka*) (expresses a denial of, or a
protest against a ridiculous statement) ← after the dictionary
form of a verb

Hanasu mono desu ka.   Of course I would not tell
     him.

Sonna koto ga aru mono desu   That is impossible!
ka.

9. *mono da* (denotes exclamatory feeling)

Hen-na koto ga aru mono desu nē. — What a strange thing does happen!

Takai kuruma o katta mono desu nē. — What an expensive car you have bought!

Jikan no tatsu no wa hayai mono da. — How time flies!

10. *mono da kara* (or *mono de*) (because)

Hayaku aruita mono da kara, kutabiremashita. — Because I walked fast, I became tired.

11. (placed at the end of a sentence signifies a slight protest or complaint and is mainly used by women)

Datte samui n desu mono. — Well, because it is cold.

12. *mono no* (or *to wa iu mono no*) (but; however) ← after a verb

Katta mono no, chittomo yomanai. — I bought it, but have never read it.

13. *mono o* (at the end of a sentence denotes a sort of the subjunctive)

Oshiete ageta mono o. — Ah, I could have taught you! (if you had asked me to do so)

nai

1. (non-existent)

Ima nai n desu. — I do not have it now.

2. (not) ← after the negative form of a verb

Nomanai deshō. — He won't drink it.

3. (not) ← after the adverbial form of a true adjective

Samukunai desu ka?   Aren't you cold?

4. *ja* (or *de wa* or *de*) *nai* (not) ← after a noun or the stem of a quasi-adjective

Nihonjin ja nai deshō.	Perhaps he is not Japanese.
Shizuka ja nakatta n desu.	It was not quiet.

5. *nai de* (without -ing) ← after the negative form of a verb

Kusuri o nomanai de nema-shita.	I went to bed without taking medicine.

The pattern *zu ni*, which is a shade less conversational, can be used in place of *nai de*.

6. *ja* (or *de*) *nai to* (if not; unless) ← after a noun or the stem of a quasi-adjective

Anata ja nai to dekimasen.	Only you can do it.
Hachiji ja nai to kaerimasen.	He won't be back before 8.
Kumori ja nai to, miemasu.	You can see it, if it is not cloudy.

The pattern *ja* (or *de*) *nakereba* can be used as a substitute for the above.

7. *ja* (or *de*) *nakute* (instead of) ← after a noun or the stem of a quasi-adjective

Kyō ja nakute ashita kite kudasai.	Please come tomorrow instead of today.

8. *nakereba naranai* (or *ikenai*) (must; should) ← after the 1st base of a verb or the adverbial form of a true adjective

Hon-ya ni yoranakereba narimasen.	I have to drop in at the book-store.
Shirokunakereba ikemasen ka?	Should it be white?

The pattern *nai to ikenai* is a substitute for the above.

64FUNCTIONAL GRAMMAR

9. *ja* (or *de*) *nakereba naranai* (or *ikenai*) (must be; should be) ← after a noun or the stem of a quasi-adjective

Chairo de nakereba ikemasen.   It should be brown.

The pattern *de* (or *ja*) *nai to ikenai* is a substitute for the above.

10. *nakereba naranaku* (or *ikenaku*) *naru* (get to the point where one has to ...) ← after the 1st base of a verb or the adverbial form of a true adjective

Tōkyō e kaeranakereba nara-naku narimashita.   Something has happened which compels me to go back to Tokyo.

11. *ja* (or *de*) *nakereba naranaku* (or *ikenaku*) *naru* (get to the point where it has to be ...) ← after a noun or the stem of a quasi-adjective

Anata de nakereba naranaku narimashita.   The situation is such that you should be the man (to do the job).

12. *nakute mo ii* (need not) ← after the 1st base of a verb or the adverbial form of a true adjective

Yomanakute mo ii deshō.   Perhaps you do not need to read it.

Yawarakakunakute mo ii n desu.   It does not need to be soft.

13. *ja* (or *de*) *nakute mo ii* (need not be) ← after a noun or the stem of a quasi-adjective

Hyaku-doru de nakute mo ii n desu.   It does not have to be $100.

14. *nakute wa ikenai* (or *naranai*) (must; should) ← after the 1st base of a verb or the adverbial form of a true adjective

Nandomo yomanakute wa ike- You must read it many times.
masen.

Haba ga hirokunakute wa ike- It has to be broad.
masen.

15. *ja* (or *de*) *nakute wa ikenai* (or *naranai*) (should be; must be) ← after a noun or the stem of a quasi-adjective

Eiwa-jisho de nakute wa ike- It has to be an English-Japa-
masen. nese dictionary.

The pattern *nakute wa naranai* is less colloquial than *nakute wa ikenai.*

naru

1. (become; grow) ← after the adverbial form of adjectives
Kuraku narimashita ne. It has become dark, hasn't it?
Jōzu-ni naru deshō. He will become good at it.

2. *ni naru* (become) ← after a noun
Kyōshi ni naru sō desu. He says he will become a teacher.

3. *ni naru* (amount to)
Minna de nisen-en ni nari- The total comes to ¥2,000.
masu.

4. *ni naru* (elapse)
Koko e kite kara sannen ni It is three years since I came
narimasu. here.

5. *o-... ni naru* (makes a verb politer) ← the 2nd base of most of Group I and II verbs precedes *ni naru*

Omachi ni narimasu ka.   Would you wait?

Go- is used instead of o- for most of *suru*-ending verbs.

Gosōdan ni narimasu ka?   Would you consult him?

6. *yō ni naru* (come to; get to the point where) ← after the dictionary form of a verb

Sugu wakaru yō ni naru de-shō.   You will soon get to the point where you can understand it.

ni

1. (to —— after the indirect object)

Anata ni agemasu.   I will give it to you.

2. (at; in —— location)

Kono heya ni arimasu ka?   Is it in this room?

3. (at —— time)

Rokuji ni okimashita.   I got up at 6.
Sangatsu ni kimasu.   He will come in March.

4. (and) ← for connecting nouns

Ringo ni momo ni nashi o tabemashita.   We ate apples, peaches and pears.

5. (at; in) (final point of a given action or motion)

Ashita no asa uchi ni tsuku d :shō.   He will get home tomorrow morning.

6. (to; for —— direction)

Shitamachi ni ikimashita.   He went downtown.

In this sense *ni* and *e* are generally interchangeable.

7. (purpose) ← after the 2nd base of a verb and followed by verbs denoting 'coming' and 'going'

Tegami o dashi ni ikimashita. He went to mail a letter.
Asobi ni kite kudasai. Come to see me, please.

8. (purpose) ← after a noun
Kore wa nan ni tsukaimasu ka? What do you use this for?
Itsu ryokō ni irasshaimasu ka? When will you go on a trip?

9. (by) (after the agent in the causative, passive, and sometimes potential constructions)

Otōto ni kutsu o migakasemashita. I made my younger brother shine my shoes.
Sensei ni homerareta sō desu. I hear he was praised by his teacher.
Kodomo ni wakarimasu ka? Can it be understood by a child?

10. (among)

Nihonjin ni sō iu hito wa mezurashikunai n desu. Such people are not rare among the Japanese.

no

1. (—'s)

Donata no desu ka? Whose is it?

2. (of)

Tōkyō Daigaku no gakusei desu. He is a student of Tokyo University.

3. (one; ones)

Akai no o misete kudasai. Show me the red one, please.
Hoka-no o kudasai. Please give me another one.

As the second example indicates, in case a *no*-ending quasi-adjective is used, *no* meaning 'one' is not added.

4. (for joining two nouns in apposition)

Chiji no Toda-san wa raishū Amerika e iku yotei desu. Mr. Toda, the Governor, is planning to go to the U.S. next week.

5. (used for making a noun out of a verb)

Sō suru no wa muzukashiku nai deshō. It may not be difficult to do so.

Irassharu no o tanoshimi ni shite imasu. I am looking forward to your coming.

K-san ga Nihongo o hanasu no o kikimashita. I heard Mr. K speak Japanese.

6. *no* (or *n*) *da* (often used at the end of a sentence just to round off the sentence) ← after a verb or a true adjective

Ima iku n desu ka? Are you going now?

Itai n desu. It hurts.

7. *na no* (or *n*) *da* ← after a noun or the stem of a quasi-adjective

Ōki-na uchi na n desu. It is a big house.

Byōki na n desu ka? Is he sick?

8. (used to connect a noun to a phrase placed attributively before it)

Rondon ni iru ani e no tegami desu. This is a letter to my elder brother who is in London.

9. (added to an adjective sometimes makes an abstract noun)

Takai no ni bikkuri-shimashita. I was surprised at it being expensive (the dearness).

Jōzu-na no wa shitte imasu. We know his skill in it.

10. (used in adjectival phrases)

me no yowai kodomo	a child with weak sight
sei no takai hito	a person of great stature
Nihongo no jōzu-na gaijin	a foreigner who has a good command of Japanese
kao no kirei-na onna	a woman with a pretty face
hari no kowareta tokei	a watch whose hand is broken

When used predicatively, *no* is changed into *ga*:

Kono obāsan wa me ga warui n desu.	This old woman has weak sight. (As for this old woman, her eyes are weak.)
Imōto-san wa sei ga takai desu ne.	Your younger sister is tall, isn't she?
Kā-san wa Nihongo ga jōzu desu.	Mr. Carr is fluent in Japanese.
Teito-san wa kao ga kirei desu ka?	Does Miss Tate have a pretty face?
Kono tokei wa hari ga kowarete imasu.	The hand of this watch is broken.

11. (employed at the end of a sentence as a colloquial substitute for *ka*)

Kaii no?	Is it itchy?
Iku no?	Are you going?
Tabeta no?	Did you eat?
Suki-na no?	Do you like it?
Amerikajin na no?	Is he American?

12. (used at the end of a sentence exclusively by women and children)

Chikai no.	It is near.
Hontō-na no.	It is true.
Ima taberu no.	I eat now.

This *no* makes sentences more emotional.

13. (used before *kamo shirenai*)

Netsu ga aru no kamo shire-   He probably has fever.
masen.

This *no* serves as (a) a sentence softener; (b) an expression implying the reason as well as conjecture.

node

1. (because) ← after a verb or a true adjective

Yakamashii node, hikkoshi-   Because it was noisy, I mov-
mashita.   ed out.
Takusan aruita node, kutabire- Because we walked a lot, we
mashita.   were tired.

Node is less frequently used than *kara*. A clause ending with *node* is more emphatic than one ending with *kara* and is more closely bound up with the rest of the sentence. *Node* is not to be used if the final clause denotes request, order, invitation, etc. *Node* is often corrupted into *nde*.

2. *na node* (because) ← after a noun or the stem of a quasi-adjective

Ame na node, ikimasen de-   Because it was rainy weather,
shita.   I did not go.
Koko wa shizuka-na node,   I like this place, because it is
suki desu.   quiet.

Na node is often shortened into *na nde*.

no de

1. (and) (used at the end of a clause after a verb or a true adjective)

Yuki no hi ni iru no de, ame   We need it on a snowy day
no hi ni wa irimasen.   and do not need it on a rainy
                                 day.

2. *na no de* (and) ← after a noun or the stem of a quasi-adjective

Kore wa kyakuma na no de, This is a drawing room, and
ima ja arimasen. not a living room.

No de and *na no de* are often shortened to *n de* and *na n de* respectively. The context determines whether *node* (because) or *no de* (and) is meant.

noni

1. (despite; although) ← after a verb or a true adjective

Kujikan neta noni, mada ne- I am still sleepy, although I
mui n desu. slept for nine hours.
Atama ga itai noni, dekake- He went out, although he had
mashita. a headache.

2. *na noni* (despite; although) ← after a noun

Hidoi ame na noni kimashita. He came in spite of the heavy
rain.

3. (I wish) ← generally after ... *to ii*

Mō sukoshi suzushii to ii noni. I wish it were a little cooler.
Yuki ga yameba (or *yamu to*) I wish it would stop snowing.
ii noni.
Motto hayaku kaereba yokat- You should have come back
ta noni. earlier.

no ni

1. (in order to) ← after the dictionary form of a verb

Shinbun o yomu no ni jisho ga Do you need a dictionary in
irimasu ka? order to read a newspaper?

o

1. (before the direct object)

Anata wa kono zasshi o doko   Where did you buy this maga-
de kaimashita ka?   zine?

The following construction is possible when the subject is
left out:

Kono zasshi wa doko de kai-   As for this magazine, where
mashita ka?   did you buy it?

2. (denotes a place of motion)

Dekoboko-michi o hashirima-   We ran along the bumpy road.
shita.

Hikōki ga sora o tonde ima-   An airplane was flying in the
shita.   air.

The postposition *o* denotes a place in which or through
which such a motion as walking, running, passing, flying, etc.
occurs.

3. (sometimes used in the passive construction)

Jitensha o dorobō ni nusuma- I had my bicycle stolen by a
remashita.   robber.

4. (often replaced by *wa* for contrast or emphasis)

Bīru wa nomimasu ga, sake   He drinks beer, but does not
wa nomimasen.   drink 'sake'.

oku

1. (put something on a place; place)

Tsukue no ue ni oite kudasai. Put it on the desk, please.

2. *-te oku* (denotes doing a thing beforehand for future need
or use)

Namae o kaite oku hō ga ii   You had better write your
deshō.   name (for future reference).

3. *-te oku* (denotes the complete settling of a matter)

Hako no ue ni oite okimashita.   I put it on the desk (and it is there).

4. *-te oku* (anyhow)

Gohyaku-en ni shite okimashō.   We will offer this for 500 yen for this occasion.

shi

(and; so) (has enumerative force and is used in connecting sentences — not words)

Yoku taberu shi, yoku nemasu.   He eats well and sleeps well.

Natsu wa atsui shi, fuyu wa samui n desu.   It is hot in summer and cold in winter.

'Hiragana' mo kakeru shi, 'kanji' mo yomemasu.   He can write 'hiragana' and can read 'kanji'.

Kore wa hade da shi, sore wa jimi da shi, dotchi mo ki ni irimasen.   This is bright and that is quiet, and neither of them takes my fancy.

Netsu ga atta shi, atama ga itakatta n desu.   I had fever and a headache.

sō

1. (so)

Sō desu ka?   Is that so?

2. *sō da* (they say; I hear) ← after true adjectives or verbs

Samui sō desu.   It is cold, I hear.

Nomu sō desu.   He drinks it i hear.

Tōkyō e itta sō desu.   I understand he went to Tokyo.

Note that *sō da* is placed at the end of a sentence.

3. *da sō da* (they say; I hear) ← after a noun or the stem of a quasi-adjective

Eigo ga jōzu da sō desu.   I hear he is fluent in English.

sō

1. (appearance; likelihood) ← after the 2nd base of verbs, the stem of adjectives or quasi-adjectives

Kono okashi wa oishi sō desu.	This cake looks good.
Ame ga furi sō desu ne.	It looks like rain, doesn't it?
Jōbu sō deshita.	He looked healthy.
Shinsetsu-sō-na otoko ga ha-nashikaketa n desu.	A kind-looking man spoke to me.

Note that *nai* (non-existent) and *yoi* (good) undergo a slight change:

Okane wa nasa sō desu.	He seems to have no money.
Yosa sō desu.	It looks good.

Compare (a) with (b):

(a) *Tsuyoi sō desu.*	It is strong, I hear.
(b) *Tsuyo sō desu.*	It looks strong.

(a) *Yuki ga furu sō desu.*	It snows, I hear.
(b) *Yuki ga furi sō desu.*	It looks like snow.

(a) *Shizuka da sō desu.*	It is quiet, I hear.
(b) *Shizuka sō desu.*	It appears quiet.

2. *sō da* (or *sō ni naru*) (be ready to; threaten to) ← after the 2nd base of a verb

Wasure sō deshita.	I almost forgot it.
Kuruma ni hikare sō ni natta n desu.	He came near being hit by a car.

3. *sō na mono* (or *mon*) *da* (should; ought to) ← after the 2nd base of verbs, the stem of true adjectives or quasi-adjectives

Wakari sō na mono desu.	He ought to understand it.
Motto yasu sō na mon desu.	It should be cheaper.

suru

1. (do)

Suki-na yō ni suru to iimashi-ta. He said he would do as he pleased.

2. (make into; make) ← after the adverbial form of adjectives

Motto chiisaku shite kudasai. Make it smaller, please.

3. *ni suru* (make into; make) ← after a noun

Chichi wa boku o isha ni suru tsumori deshita. Father planned to make a doctor of me.

Dareka ga midori ni shita n desu. Somebody turned it green.

4. (cost)

Ikura shimashita ka? How much did it cost you?

5. (elapse)

Gofun shitara, keshite kudasai. Please turn it off five minutes later.

6. (used in verbalizing a noun)

Benkyō-suru hō ga ii. You had better study.

Some other examples are: *sanpo* (a walk)—*sanpo-suru* (take a walk), *hakken* (discovery)—*hakken-suru* (discover), *chūkoku* (advice)—*chūkoku-suru* (advise), etc.

7. (used after *ga* or *wa,* meaning 'feel')

Memai ga shimashita. I felt dizzy.

Kiita toki, donna kimochi ga shita n desu ka? How did you feel, when you heard it?

Some other examples are: *ki ga suru* (feel), *samuke ga*

suru (feel a chill), *zutsū ga suru* (have a headache), *aji ga suru* (taste), *nioi ga suru* (smell), *koe ga suru* (a voice is heard), *oto ga suru* (a sound is heard), etc.

8. *koto ni suru* (decide to) ← after the dictionary form of a verb

Kono uchi o kariru koto ni shimashita.	I have decided to rent this house.

9. *ni suru* (decide on) ← after a noun

Sono hi ni shimashō.	Let's decide on that date.

10. *ni* (or *to*) *shite wa* (considering; for)

Ima goro ni shite wa chotto samusugimasu.	It is a little cold for this time of the year.

11. *o-... suru* (humble) ← o- precedes the 2nd base of most verbs belonging to Group I and II.

Otsutsumi shimashō ka?	Shall I wrap it?

12. *tari, tari suru* (now .... and then ....; sometimes .... and sometimes ....)

Ame ga futtari, yandari shite imashita.	It was raining on and off.
Kodomotachi wa hon o yondari, terebi o mitari, sanposhitari shimashita.	Some of the children read books, some watched tv, and some took a walk.

The frequentative form, which denotes (a) acts or states occurring alternately and (b) a distributive sense, is generally used in pairs or more, with the last member followed by *suru*. The frequentative form is obtained by the repetition of the plain past form of verbs followed by *ri*.

13. *to suru* (suppose that)

Ima iku to shimashō.	Let's assume that we go now.
Ashita tenki da to shite, ...	On the assumption that it is fine weather tomorrow, ...

14. *to suru* (be about to; try to; intend) ← after the volitional form of a verb

Tegami o kakō to shimashita.	I was about to write a letter.
Dekakeyō to shita toki ni, kimashita.	He came when I was about to go out.
Mado o akeyō to shite, ochimashita.	He fell in an attempt to open the window.

The volitional form is obtained as follows:

(a) Group I verbs:

Dictionary form	Volitional form
yobu (call)	*yobō*
oyogu (swim)	*oyogō*
aruku (walk)	*arukō*
nomu (drink)	*nomō*
shinu (die)	*shinō*
kaeru (return)	*kaerō*
hairu (enter)	*hairō*
toru (take)	*torō*
hanasu (speak)	*hanasō*
tatsu (stand)	*tatō*
kau (buy)	*kaō*

Replace the final *u* by *ō*.

(b) Group II verbs:

taberu (eat)	*tabeyō*
miru (see)	*miyō*

Replace the final *ru* by *yō*.

(c) Irregular verbs:

kuru (come)	*koyō*

suru (do)　　　　　　　　　　*shiyō*

15. *wa suru ga, ...* (emphatic) ← after the 2nd base of a verb

Yomi wa shimasu ga, imi wa wakaranai n desu.　He certainly reads it, but does not understand it.

Kake wa shinai n desu ga, yomeru n desu.　I cannot write it; however I can read it.

te-form

A non-final verb (verbs) or true adjective (adjectives) must be changed into the *te*-form. A non-final quasi-adjective (quasi-adjectives) must be changed into the *de*-form.

1. (and; but)

Tabete nomimashita.　We ate and drank.

Yomete, hanasete, kakemasu.　He can read, speak, and write it.

Samukute, nemuremasen deshita.　It was cold and I could not sleep.

Jōbu de anmari takakunai n desu.　It is durable and (but) not too expensive.

As is indicated above, the final verb determines the tense.

2. (because)

Zutsū ga shite, benkyō dekinakatta n desu.　I had a headache; so I could not study.

Atsukute, ikitakunai to itte imasu.　He says that he does not feel like going, because it is hot.

Heta de hazukashii n desu.　I am so poor at it that I am ashamed of myself.

The context determines whether the *te*-form means 'and', 'but' or 'because'.

3. *te mo* (even if) (becomes *de mo* when used after a quasi-adjective)

Futte mo, kimasu.	Even if it rains, I will come.
Takakute mo, kawanakereba naranai n desu.	Even if it is expensive, I have to buy it.
Binbō de mo, shōjiki desu.	He is honest, even though he is poor.

4. *te mo ii* (may —— permission)

Haitte mo ii desu ka?	May I come in?
Furukute mo ii sō desu.	He says an old one will do.
Heta de mo ii n desu.	Even if you are poor at it, it is all right.

Mo is sometimes dropped.

5. *te wa ikenai* (or *dame da, naranai*) (must not)

Enpitsu de kaite wa ikemasen.	You must not write in pencil.
Shirokute wa ikemasen.	It should not be white.
Fushinsetsu de wa ikemasen.	One should not be unkind.

Te wa and *de wa* are shortened into *tcha* and *ja* respectively in familiar speech. The pattern *te wa naranai* is bookish.

6. *nakute mo ii* (need not) ← after the negative form of verbs or adjectives

Isoganakute mo ii n desu.	You do not have to hurry.
Akakunakute mo ii deshō.	Perhaps it does not have to be red.
Shizuka de nakute mo ii sō desu.	It does not have to be quiet, I hear.

Mo is sometimes left out.

7. *nakute wa ikenai* (or *dame da, naranai*) (must; should) ← after the negative form of verbs or adjectives

Itsu made ni kakanakute wa ikemasen ka?	By when should I write it?

Chiisakunakute wa ikenai n desu.	It should be small.
Kenkō de nakute wa ikenai n desu.	One must be healthy.

8. *te ageru* (give a favor of -ing)

Kaite agemasu.	I will write it for you.
Kaite sashiagemasu.	„ (polite)
Kaite yarimasu.	„ (non-polite)

9. *te aru* ('-ing' is completed)

Hako ni irete arimasu ka?	Is it put in the box?

10. *te goran nasai* (try to)

Kono fuku o kite goran na-sai.	Just try this suit on.
Tabete goran nasai.	Eat and see how it tastes.

Note the difference in the degree of politeness in the following:

(a) *Kaite kudasai.*	Please write.
(b) *Kaite goran nasai.*	Just write. Try writing.
(c) *Kaki nasai.*	Write.
(d) *Kake.*	Write!

11. *te iku* (keep on)

Kō iu fū ni shite iku tsumori desu.	I intend to keep on doing like this.

12. *te iru* (be -ing)

Yasunde imasu.	He is resting.
Asa wa harete imashita.	It was clear in the morning.
Musume wa hon o yonde ori-masu.	My daughter is reading a book. (humble)
Donata o matte irasshaimasu ka?	Whom are you waiting for? (polite)

13. *te kudasai* (please do ....)

Yukkuri hanashite kudasai.	Please speak slowly.
Misete chōdai.	Show it to me, please. (familiar)

14. *te kureru* (be given a favor of -ing)

Musuko ga itte kuremashita.	My son went there for me.
Goshujin ga motte kite kudasaimashita.	Your husband was kind enough to bring it to me. (polite)

15. *te kuru* (do something and come; go and do something; become; grow)

Aruite kimashita.	I came on foot.
	He walked towards you.
Mite kimashō ka?	Shall I go and see it?
Samuku natte kuru deshō.	It will become cold.

16. *te miru* (do something and see; try to)

Tabete mimasen ka?	Won't you eat and see how it tastes?
Yatte mimashita.	I had a try at it.

17. *te morau* (receive a favor of -ing)

Matte morai tai n desu.	I want you to wait.
Ashita denwa-shite itadakemasu ka?	Could I have you call me tomorrow?

18. *te oku* (do something beforehand)

Hanashite oku hō ga ii deshō.	You had better tell him about it beforehand.
Kaite okimashita.	I have written it (for future reference or need).

19. *te shimau* (finish -ing)

Wasurete shimaimashita.   I forgot it completely.

to

1. (and)

Kyō to ashita uchi ni imasu.   I will be at home today and tomorrow.

Note that *to* cannot be used for connecting clauses.

2. (with; together)

Tomodachi to ikimashita.   I went with a friend of mine.

3. (that ....)

Kuru to iimashita.   He said that he would come.

Compare (a) with (b):

(a) *Yomu to omoimasu.*   I think he will read it.
(b) *Yomō to omoimasu.*   I think I will read it.

Take note of the two different subjects in (a) and the same subjects in (b). The expression *to omou* used after a verb in the future tense denotes 'intention', if the subjects of the two verbs are the same; however, if the subjects are different, it means 'think', 'hope', 'fear', etc. For the above reason *yomō*, which is the volitional form of *yomu*, is used in (b).

4. (after " ")

"Kumotte iru." to iimashita.   He said, "It is cloudy."

5. (whenever; when; if) ← after the dictionary form of a verb or a true adjective

Haru ga kuru to, sakimasu.   When spring comes, they bloom.

Kono hana wa samui to, kare-   This flower withers, if it is
masu.   cold.
Sake o nomu to, nemashita.   Whenever he drank 'sake', he
                                         fell into sleep.

Note that even if the verb in the principal clause is in the
past tense, the verb preceding *to* is in the present tense.

6. *da* (or *desu*) *to* (whenever; when; if) ← after a noun or
    the stem of a quasi-adjective

Ame da to, ichijikan ijō kaka-   If it is rainy weather, it will
ru deshō.   take over one hour.

7. *to iu koto* (the fact that)

Nyūin-shite ita to iu koto wa   I did not know that he had
shiranakatta n desu.   been in hospital.
Sugu sumu to iu koto o kiki-   I heard that he would finish it
mashita.   soon.

8. *to iu no* (that which is called)

Han to iu no wa nan desu ka?   What does that which is call-
                                         ed 'han' mean?

9. *to ka* (to the effect that)

Rainen kuru to ka itte imasu.   He says to the effect that he
                                         will come next year.

10. *toka* (and; or; such as)

Hon toka zasshi toka wa ka-   Put books, magazines, and
ban ni irenasai.   such in your briefcase.

11. *... to ... to,* (comparison)

Kore to sore to, dotchi ga ii   Which is better, this or that?
desu ka?
Gyū to buta to tori to, dore ga   Which do you like best, beef,
ichiban osuki desu ka?   pork or chicken?

tokoro

1. (place)

Koko wa sumi-ii tokoro desu.	This is a nice place to live in.
Sonna tokoro da.	That is just about it.

2. *tokoro da* (be about to; be on the point of) ← after the dictionary form of a verb

Dekakeru tokoro desu.	I am about to take off.
Uru tokoro deshita.	He was on the point of selling it.

3. *tokoro da* (did something just now) ← after the plain past form of a verb

Denpō o utta tokoro desu.	I have just sent a telegram.

4. *te iru tokoro da* (be in the process of -ing)

Ofuro ni haitte iru tokoro de-su.	He is taking a bath now.
Anata no koto o hanashite ita tokoro desu.	We were just talking about you.

5. *tokoro e* (while; when; just as)

Yūhan o tabete iru tokoro e, kimashita.	He came while I was eating supper.
Ryokō kara kaetta tokoro e, kyaku ga kita n desu.	A guest came just when I got back from my trip.
Ii tokoro e irasshaimashita.	You came in the nick of time.
Samukatta tokoro e, kaze ga fuite, motto samuku natta n desu.	When it was already cold, because it blew, it became much colder.

6. *tokoro o* (when; while)

Oisogashii tokoro o ojama-shimashita.	Excuse me for disturbing you when you were busy.

7. *tokoro de* (even though) ← after the plain past form of a verb

Yonda tokoro de, wakaranai deshō.

Even if I read it, I could not understand it.

Kuruma ga atta tokorode, ikanakatta deshō.

Even if he had had a car, he would not have gone there.

Note that this pattern is used in connection with the subjunctive.

8. *Tokoro de* (by the way) ← at the top of a sentence

Tokoro de, itsu hajimaru n desu ka?

By the way, when will it begin?

9. *tokoro ga* (but; and yet; contrary to expectation) ← after the plain past form of a verb

Tazuneta tokoro ga, ainiku rusu deshita.

I visited him, but unluckily he was not at home.

10. *Tokoro ga* (however; but) ← at the top of a sentence

Tokoro ga, dame deshita.

It, however, was in vain.

11. *dokoro ka* (far from; to say nothing of) ← after the dictionary form of a verb, a true adjective, the stem of a quasi-adjective or a noun

Gakkari-suru dokoro ka, yorokobimashita.

Far from being discouraged, he was glad.

Nurui dokoro ka, atsui desu yo.

Far from lukewarm, it is hot, I tell you.

Kanji dokoro ka, hiragana mo kakenai n desu.

He cannot write 'hiragana', much less 'kanji'.

Kono nekutai wa hade dokoro ka, jimi desu.

This necktie is far from loud; it is quiet.

wa

1. (after the subject)

Ano kata wa Toyoda-san desu.   He is Mr. Toyoda.

2. (as for)

Kono shūkanshi wa kinjo no   I bought this weekly maga-
    hon-ya de kaimashita.   zine at the bookstore in my
                                  neighborhood. (As for this
                                  weekly magazine, I bought
                                  it at the bookstore in my
                                  neighborhood.)

3. (commonly used in a negative sentence)

Kyō wa getsuyō ja arimasen.   Today is not Monday.

4. (emphatic)

Muzukashiku wa nai n desu.   It is not difficult.

5. (contrast—explicit or implied)

Kono machi wa yakamashii   This town is noisy, but my
    desu ga, watakushi no kokyō   home town is quiet.
    wa shizuka desu.
Watakushi wa ikimasu.   I will go (he may go or not).

6. te wa (if)

Hikui koe de hanashite wa,   If you talk in a low voice, I
    kikoemasen.   cannot hear.
Takakute wa, kaitakunai n   If it is expensive, I do not
    desu.   want to buy it.
Hontō de wa, komarimasu.   If it is true, I will be in
                             trouble.

    Note that the principal clause generally carries an un-
favorable connotation.

Compare (a) with (b):

(a) *Anmari nonde wa, kara-*   If you drink too much, it will
    da ni warui deshō.   be bad for you.

(b) *Anmari nonde, atama ga*   Because I drank too much, I
    itai n desu.   have a headache.

(a) *Furukute wa, dame desu.*   If it is old, it won't do.

(b) *Furukute, dame desu.*   Because it is old, it won't do.
                           (It is old and won't do.)

7. (used for indicating the topic of a sentence)

Koko wa (or *de wa*) *imagoro*   Does it snow in here about
    yuki ga furimasu ka?   this time of the year?

8. *wa suru* (emphatic) ← after the 2nd base of a verb

Yomi wa shimasu ga, hanase-   I do read it, but cannot speak
    nai n desu.   it.

9. (female expression) ← at the end of a sentence

Sukoshi ōkisugiru wa.   It's a little too big.

wake

1. (reason; cause)

Sono wake wa kō desu.   The reason is this.

2. *wake ga aru* (there is reason)

Nanika wake ga arimasu ka?   Is there any reason for that?

3. *wake wa nai* (it is impossible that ...; cannot; there is no reason)

Sonna-ni takai wake wa nai   It cannot be that expensive, I
    sō desu.   hear.

Betsu-ni wake wa nai n desu.   There is no special reason for
                           that.

4. *wake da* (mean)

Henji o kakanakute mo ii wake desu ka?	Does it mean that I do not have to write a reply?
Kimi ga machigatte iru to iu wake ja nai.	I do not mean to say that you are in the wrong.

5. *wake ni wa ikanai* (cannot very well) ← after the dictionary form of a verb

Shōtai o kotowaru wake ni wa ikanai n desu.	I cannot very well decline the invitation.
Sō iu wake ni wa mairimasen.	We cannot very well do so.

6. *nai wake ni wa ikanai* (cannot help but) ← after the negative form of a verb

Warawanai wake ni wa ikimasen deshita.	I could not help laughing.

The pattern *zaru o enai* after the negative form of a verb, which is less colloquial, can be used as a substitute for *nai wake ni wa ikanai*.

Wa before *ikanai* in 5. and 6. is sometimes left out.

yō

1. *yō da* (seem; appear) ← after verbs or true adjectives

Maiasa kuru yō desu.	He seems to come every morning.
Wasureta yō desu.	They appear to have forgotten it.
Soko wa samui yō desu.	It seems to be cold there.

2. *no yō da* (appear; look like) ← after a noun

Anata no kuruma no yō desu ne.	It looks like your car, doesn't it?

3. *no* (or *na*) *yō da* (appear; look like) ← after the stem of quasi-adjectives

Kono tenki wa futsū-no yō desu.   This weather seems normal.

Fushigi-na yō desu.   It looks mysterious.

4. *yō na* (like; such as) ← after verbs or true adjectives

Uso o iu yō na hito ja nai de- shō.   I do not think he is the type of a man who tells a lie.

Takai yō na koto o itte ima- shita.   He said that it would probably be expensive.

5. *no yō na* (like; such as) ← after a noun

Yūbin-ya-san no yō na hito ga tatte imasu.   A man who looks like a mailman is standing.

6. *no* (or *na*) *yō na* (like; such as) ← after the stem of quasi-adjectives

Atarimae-no yō na kao o shite imashita.   He wore a look of no surprise.

7. *yō ni* (like; in such a way as) ← after verbs or true adjectives

Iwareta yō ni shita n desu.   I did as I was told.

Ii yō ni shite kudasai.   Please do as you like.

8. *no yō ni* (like; in such a way as) ← after a noun

Nihonjin no yō ni Nihongo ga hanasemasu.   She can speak Japanese like a native.

9. *no* (or *na*) *yō ni* (like; in such a way as) ← after the stem of quasi-adjectives

Fushigi-na yō ni naorimashi- ta.   I was cured like a miracle.

10. *yō ni* (so as to) ← after the dictionary form of a verb

Chotto matsu yō ni itte kuda-   Won't you please tell him to
sai masen ka?   wait a second?
Wakaru yō ni yukkuri hana-   I talked slowly so that he
shimashita.   might understand.

11. *yō ni naru* (get to the point where ....; come to) ← after
the dictionary form of a verb

Hanaseru yō ni narimashita.   He got to the point where he
                                    is able to speak it.

12. *yō ni suru* (try to) ← after the dictionary form of a verb

Getsumatsu made ni owaru   Please try to finish it by the
yō ni shite kudasai.   end of this month.

13. (I tell you; I assure you) ← at the end of a sentence

Oishii yo.   It sure is delicious.
Oishii wa yo.   „   (used by women)

Compound Verbs

There are a great number of compound verbs which are
formed by the addition of one verb to the 2nd base of another.
Those in common use are as follows:

-*agaru* (ascend)   *deki-agaru* (be completed); *tobi-*
                              agaru (jump)
-*ageru* (raise)   *hiroi-ageru* (pick up); *tsumi-ageru*
                              (pile up)
-*akiru* (become tired of)   *kiki-akiru* (become tired of hear-
                              ing)
-*ataru* (hit)   *omoi-ataru* (call to mind); *tsuki-*
                              ataru (bump against; come to the
                              end)

-ateru (hit)	*ii-ateru* (guess); *oshi-ateru* (push something against)
-atsumeru (gather)	*haki-atsumeru* (sweep up); *yobi-atsumeru* (call together)
-au (meet)	*hanashi-au* (talk with); *tasuke-au* (help each other)
-awaseru (join)	*ari-awaseru* (happen to have); *kumi-awaseru* (combine)
-chigaeru (mistake)	*kaki-chigaeru* (miswrite); *yomi-chigaeru* (misread)
-dasu (begin, put out)	*furi-dasu* (begin raining, snowing); *tsumami-dasu* (drag out)
-deru (come out)	*shimi-deru* (ooze out); *waki-deru* (gush out)
-hajimeru (begin)	*furi-hajimeru* (begin raining, snowing); *kaki-hajimeru* (begin to write)
-hanasu (release)	*ake-hanasu* (leave something open); *dashippanasu* (leave something lying about)
-hateru (exhaust)	*komari-hateru* (be at one's wit's end); *tsukare-hateru* (be dead tired)
-hazusu (remove)	*tori-hazusu* (remove)
-ireru (put in)	*kaki-ireru* (fill in); *nage-ireru* (throw in)
-iru (go in)	*kiki-iru* (listen attentively); *tachi-iru* (meddle in; enter)
-kaeru (change)	*nori-kaeru* (transfer); *tori-kaeru* (exchange)
-kaesu (return)	*tori-kaesu* (regain); *yomi-kaesu* (re-read)
-kakaru (come to; be ready)	*de-kakaru* (be about to come out); *tōri-kakaru* (happen to pass by)
-kakeru (begin)	*ii-kakeru* (begin speaking); *tabe-*

-*kawaru* (change)

-*kesu* (erase)

-*kiru* (cut)

-*koeru* (go over)

-*komu* (enter)

-*kosu* (exceed)

-*mawaru* (go round)

-*mawasu* (turn round)

-*naosu* (mend)

-*narabu* (line up)

-*nareru* (become accus-
tomed)

-*nokoru* (remain)

-*nokosu* (leave behind)

-*nuku* (go through)

-*oeru* (finish)

-*okosu* (raise)

-*owaru* (finish; end)

kakeru (begin to eat)
umare-kawaru (be reborn)
fuki-kesu (blow something out);
tori-kesu (cancel)
komari-kiru (be at one's wit's end);
yomi-kiru (finish reading)
nori-koeru (tide over; go over)
kangae-komu (be absorbed in
thought); *tobi-komu* (jump into)
nori-kosu (ride beyond one's desti-
nation); *tōri-kosu* (go past)
aruki-mawaru (walk about); *tobi-
mawaru* (romp about)
mi-mawasu (look around); *nori-
mawasu* (drive about)
nuri-naosu (repaint); *yari-naosu*
(do over again)
i-narabu (sit in a row); *tachi-
narabu* (stand in a row)
mi-nareru (become accustomed to
seeing); *tsukai-nareru* (get used
to using)
i-nokoru (remain behind); *ure-
nokoru* (remain unsold)
kaki-nokosu (leave a note); *tabe-
nokosu* (leave the dish unfinish-
ed)
kangae-nuku (think over); *komari-
nuku* (be at one's wit's end)
kaki-oeru (finish writing); *yomi-
oeru* (finish reading)
furi-okosu (arouse); *maki-okosu*
(stir up)
hanashi-owaru (finish talking);
yomi-owaru (finish reading)

-*sagaru* (go down)	*hiki-sagaru* (retire); *tare-sagaru* (dangle)
-*sokonau* (ruin)	*iki-sokonau* (fail to go); *mi-sokonau* (fail to see)
-*sugiru* (exceed)	*hataraki-sugiru* (overwork oneself); *tabe-sugiru* (overeat)
-*tomeru* (keep)	*hiki-tomeru* (detain); *kaki-tomeru* (write down)
-*toru* (take)	*hiki-toru* (take over); *uke-toru* (receive)
-*tōsu* (continue)	*naki-tōsu* (keep crying); *yari-tōsu* (complete)
-*tsuku* (be attached)	*kami-tsuku* (b i t e); *sui-tsuku* (stick)
-*tsukusu* (exhaust)	*tsukai-tsukusu* (use up); *yaki-tsukusu* (burn up)
-*tsuzukeru* (continue)	*hanashi-tsuzukeru* (continue talking); *tobi-tsuzukeru* (continue flying)
-*tsuzuku* (continue)	*furi-tsuzuku* (continue raining, snowing); *teri-tsuzuku* (continue shining)
-*wasureru* (forget)	*ii-wasureru* (forget to mention); *kaki-wasureru* (forget to write)

There are, in addition to compound verbs, some compound adjectives which are formed by the addition of an adjective to the 2nd base of a verb.

-*ii* (good)	*hanashi-ii* (easy to talk to); *wakari-ii* (easy to understand)
-*kurushii* (painful)	*kiki-gurushii* (offensive to the ear); *mi-gurushii* (unsightly)
-*nikui* (hard)	*kiri-nikui* (hard to cut); *yomi-nikui* (hard to read)

-yasui (easy) *nomi-yasui* (easy to drink); *tsuku-ri-yasui* (easy to make)

The true adjectives-*ii* and *-yoi* are interchangeable, the latter being less colloquial.

Respect Expressions

Broadly speaking, the Japanese custom demands that, in case respect is to be shown, the 1st person should use humble words when he refers to his actions and things and polite words when he refers to the actions and things of the 2nd person as well as the 3rd person.

I Verbs

Plain	Humble	Honorific
ageru (offer)	*sashiageru*	*sashiageru*
aru (have; exist)	*gozaimasu* (*gozaru*)	*gozaimasu*
au (meet)	*ome ni kakaru; oai suru*	*oai ni naru*
desu (be)	*de gozaimasu*	*de gozaimasu*
hanasu (tell)	*mōsu; mōshiageru; ohanashi suru*	*ossharu* (*osshaimasu*)
iku (go)	*mairu*	*irassharu* (*irasshaimasu*)
iru (be; exist)	*oru*	*irassharu; oide ni naru*
iu (say)	*mōsu; mōshi-ageru*	*ossharu*
kiku (hear; inquire)	*ukagau; oukagai suru*	*okiki ni naru*
kuru (come)	*mairu*	*irassharu; oide ni naru*
miru (see)	*haiken suru*	*goran ni naru*
miseru (show)	*ome ni kakeru; omise suru*	*omise suru*
morau (receive)	*itadaku*	*omorai ni naru*
nomu (drink)	*itadaku; chōdai suru*	*meshiagaru; agaru*
omou (think)	*zonjiru*	*o-omoi ni naru*

shiru (know)	*zonjiru*	*gozonji desu; gozonji de gozaimasu; gozonji de irassharu*
suru (do)	*itasu*	*nasaru (nasaimasu)*
taberu (eat)	*itadaku; chōdai suru*	*meshiagaru; agaru*
tazuneru (inquire)	*ukagau; otazune suru*	*otazune ni naru*
tazuneru (visit)	*ukagau; agaru; otazune suru*	*otazune ni naru*
yaru (give)	*sashiageru; ageru*	*kudasaru (kudasaimasu)* —for 1st person; *oyari ni naru*—not for 1st person
te iru (be -ing)	*te oru*	*te irassharu*
te aru ('-ing' is completed)	*te gozaimasu*	*te gozaimasu*

Compare (a) with (b):

(a) *D-san ni oai ni narimashita ka?* Have you met Mr. D?

(b) *Kesa ome ni kakarimashita.* I met him this morning.

(a) *Itsu irasshaimasu ka?* When are you going?

(b) *Ashita mairimasu.* I will go tomorrow.

(a) *Onamae wa nan to osshaimasu ka?* What is your name, please?

(b) *Yamasa to mōshimasu.* My name is Yamasa.

(a) *Goran ni narimashita ka?* Did you see it?

(b) *Haiken shimashita.* I saw it.

(a) *Gozonji desu ka?* Do you know him?

(b) *Zonjimasen.* I do not know him.

(a) *Meshiagarimasu ka?* Would you eat (drink) it?

(b) *Itadakimasu.* I will eat (drink) it.

(a) *Itsu nasaimashita ka?* When did you do it?

(b) *Sendatte itashimashita.* I did it the other day.

(a) *Kaite irasshaimasu ka?*   Are you writing?
(b) *Kaite orimasu.*   I am writing.

II Adjectives

Most of the true adjectives and quasi-adjectives except for those of Chinese origin can be made honorific by prefixing *o*. Most of those quasi-adjectives which are of Chinese origin can be made honorific by prefixing *go*.

Osamui desu ne.	It is cold, isn't it?
Oshizuka-na kata desu.	He is a quiet person.
Gorippa-na ie desu.	It is a lavish house.

When *gozaimasu*, which is the polite form of *desu*, is used with true adjectives, the following euphonic changes occur:

akai desu.	*akō gozaimasu.* (ai→ō)
samui desu.	*samū gozaimasu.* (ui→ū)
shiroi desu.	*shirō gozaimasu.* (oi→ō)
ōkii desu.	*ōkyū gozaimasu.* (kii→kyū)
atarashii desu.	*atarashū gozaimasu.* (shii→shū)

III Nouns

Humble	Honorific
chichi (father)	*otōsan; otōsama*
haha (mother)	*okāsan; okāsama*
oji (uncle)	*ojisan; ojisama*
oba (aunt)	*obasan; obasama*
shujin (husband)	*goshujin; goshujin-sama;* *dannasama*
kanai (wife)	*okusan; okusama*
musuko (son)	*botchan; musukosan*
musume (daughter)	*ojōsan; musumesan*
ani (elder brother)	*niisan; oniisan*
ane (elder sister)	*nēsan; onēsan*
otōto (younger brother)	*otōtosan*

imōto (younger sister)	*imōtosan; oimōtosan*
kodomo (child)	*kodomosan*

Compare (a) with (b):

(a) *Kono mise de okusan ni ome ni kakarimashita.* I saw your wife at this store.

(b) *Kanai wa byōki de nete orimasu.* My wife is sick in bed.

(a) *Botchan wa nannensei desu ka?* What grade is your son in?

(b) *Musuko wa ichinensei desu.* My son is in grade one.

(a) *Ano kata no ojōsan wa mō kekkon-shita n desu.* His daughter is already married.

(b) *Musume wa soto de asonde imasu .* My daughter is playing outdoors now.

O and *go*, honorific prefixes, are used in converting a great number of nouns into honorifics. However, the honorific idea is sometimes vague: *onaka* (stomach), *ocha* (tea), *gohan* (meal; cooked rice), *goten* (mansion), etc. *Go* is generally used with those nouns which are of Chinese origin: *gokeikaku* (your plan), *gokenkyū* (your research), *goryokō* (your trip), etc.

Compare (a) with (b):

(a) *Otegami arigatō gozaimashita.* Thank you for your letter.

(b) *Kinō tegami o santsū kakimashita.* I wrote three letters yesterday.

(a) *Natsuyasumi no gokeikaku wa dekimashita ka?* Have you made your plans for the summer vacation?

(b) *Keikaku o sukoshi kaeru kamo shiremasen.* I may perhaps change my plan a little.

Transitive and Intransitive Verbs

Those transitive and intransitive verb endings which are commonly met with are listed below. They may be of help towards distinguishing transitive verbs from intransitive verbs. Furthermore, it should be mentioned that quite a few verbs are used both transitively and intransitively.

Transitive	Intransitive
1. *eru*	*aru*
ageru (raise)	*agaru* (go up)
atsumeru (collect)	*atsumaru* (something gathers)
hajimeru (begin)	*hajimaru* (something begins)
kaeru (change)	*kawaru* (something changes)
kakeru (hang up)	*kakaru* (something hangs)
kimeru (decide)	*kimaru* (something is decided)
sageru (lower)	*sagaru* (go down)
shimeru (close)	*shimaru* (something closes)
tomeru (stop)	*tomaru* (something stops)
2. *eru*	*u*
akeru (open)	*aku* (something opens)
mukeru (turn; direct)	*muku* (something turns)
naraberu (display; arrange)	*narabu* (be displayed; stand in a line)
tateru (erect)	*tatsu* (stand)
tsuzukeru (continue)	*tsuzuku* (something continues)
3. *asu*	*eru*
dasu (put out)	*deru* (come out; go out)
narasu (accustom)	*nareru* (become accustomed)
tokasu (dissolve)	*tokeru* (something dissolves)
4. *yasu*	*eru*
fuyasu (increase)	*fueru* (something increases)
hiyasu (cool)	*hieru* (something grows cold)

5. *asu*   *u*

    herasu (decrease)   *heru* (something decreases)

    kawakasu (dry)   *kawaku* (become dry)

6. *asu*   *iru*

    korasu (punish)   *koriru* (learn by experience)

7. *su*   *ru*

    kaesu (return something)   *kaeru* (come back)

    mawasu (turn something   *mawaru* (go round)
    round)

    naosu (repair; cure)   *naoru* (get well; be repaired)

    nokosu (leave behind)   *nokoru* (remain)

8. *osu*   *iru*

    okosu (wake somebody   *okiru* (wake up)
    up)

    otosu (drop something)   *ochiru* (fall)

9. *su*   *reru*

    kakusu (hide something)   *kakureru* (hide)

    kobosu (spill)   *koboreru* (be spilled)

    yogosu (soil)   *yogoreru* (become soiled)

10. *u*   *eru*

    waru (break; divide)   *wareru* (something breaks)

    toru (take; get)   *toreru* (come off)

11. *u*   *aru*

    fusagu (block)   *fusagaru* (be blocked)

    sasu (sting)   *sasaru* (be stung)